HISTORY OF FORMULA ONE

BUDDH
INTERNATIONAL
CIRCUIT
INDIA'S RACING ARENA
BUDDH
INTERNATIONAL
CIRCUIT
MP
15
PETRONAS

HISTORY OF FORMULA ONE

THE CIRCUS COMES TO INDIA

Chetan Narula

Facing page: Nico Rosberg at the Formula One, Buddh International Circuit, India 2011

Lustre Press
Roli Books

CONTENTS

Facing page: Turkish Grand Prix 2009 starting grid

INDIA AND FORMULA ONE

2011

Day One: Thursday, 27 October

There is a festive feeling here in India. Not just because this week is the biggest celebration on the calendar, the festival of lights, Deepawali, but also because the biggest show on earth has landed. Yes, Formula One has finally come to town and the inaugural Indian Grand Prix is now only a couple of days away.

It hasn't been easy. 1993 was the year when F1 images were first broadcast on televisions here, and since then, it has been a dream in the making. Late in the nineties and early in the past decade, there were efforts afoot to get the race here – first in Hyderabad, then in Mumbai; later, an idea for a street race in New Delhi was also mooted. But all that is history now, for the present beckons fans from across the country, and from all over the world, to Greater Noida, seventy-odd kilometres away from the heart of the national capital.

On Thursday, the Buddh International Circuit truly came alive as all the teams, with their drivers, mechanics, and their entourages, landed. Before the storm though, came the lull, as the day started off slowly. Much of it has to do with the circuit's distance from the city; it is a proper, unchartered territory, even for trained cab and bus drivers. Once you get in though, it is a different story. The Indian tricolour beams at you from every possible angle. It is quite simply the theme of the entire circuit. From the hoardings and banners that are displayed as soon as your vehicle enters Noida, to the flags hoisted on gates and light-towers encircling the proposed Jaypee sports city, and to the paddock building itself, it is the Indian Grand Prix. You just know it!

The facility has a touch of world class about it, and many

Formula One comes to India, 2011

Previous pages: A young Indian fan at the Formula One Grand Prix

Lady Gaga's appearance during a press conference on 28 October 2011 in New Delhi. She gave a performance for India's maiden Formula One Grand Prix, 2011

team personnel have acknowledged that Korea 2010 has been trumped. Of course there were a few hiccups in the day. Power was a bit of a concern, going off a couple of times. Then there were the twin bats flying around in the media centre, but one of the many foreign journalists put it down to the 'Incredible India' experience. Focus then moved on to the drivers who were now coming out of the team buildings in full force. The press conference was lively. Rubens Barrichello talked about having an internet-based simulator at home, gifted to him by fellow countryman, Felipe Massa. The most experienced hand claimed he clocked a quicker time than his team-mate Pastor Maldonado did in the Williams simulator, for the Indian GP circuit. Chandhok was the leading hand there, explaining carefully the different duties of all the personnel involved, and how, for a small team, getting sponsorship is of utmost importance for them to develop. And no, he didn't seem disappointed at all about the team's decision; in fact, was raring to go out early on Friday morning to impress one and all.

The other Indian driver in the paddock, Narain Karthikeyan, will race on Sunday. t makes one wonder what attention Force India might have achieved if they had an Indian driver. The strain of doing umpteen promotional activities for the only Indian F1 team on the grid showed on Adrian Sutil's face. And on being asked about it, one of their mechanics did mention that 'doing well here was of prime importance to the team.' Force India will be announcing of the results of their 'One from a Billion' competition – search for young Indian drivers who could graduate to F1 – during this event. Clearly, their team principal, Vijay Mallya, wants to make an impact.

Michael Schumacher, meanwhile, remains a firm fan favourite. Not many Indians have gotten over his Ferrari days, and when I asked him about winning again, this time with Mercedes GP, he said, 'it is important for the team to develop a good car, I would like to do that (win) sooner rather than later.'

Day Two: Friday, 28 October

You can say that animals have ruled the mornings in the Indian Grand Prix so far. It were the twin bats in the media centre on Thursday and on Friday, when a Formula One engine roared in anger for the first time at the Buddh International Circuit, a stray dog found it fit to bring out the first red flag after only five minutes in the morning practice session.

Ground hogs rule the roost in Canada, so F1 is no stranger to such incidents. And the important part was that the circuit was now completely ready to host the inaugural Indian Grand Prix, minor glitches having all been taken care of.

Adrian Sutil was first out as the lights went green for first practice. Karun Chandhok was next, and then followed Narain Karthkiyen and Paul Di Resta. It was a moment for the cameras indeed, but the fight for honours had only just begun. Chandhok cheekily overtook Sutil on his outlap and set the first time, putting his name in history books. But 1:52.148 was hardly going to stand, and Karthikeyan bettered that soon enough,

F1 drivers and team bosses pay their respects with a minute's silence for Indycar driver, Dan Wheldon and Moto GP rider, Marco Simoncelli before the Indian Formula One Grand Prix 2011

when the dog allowed the session to go green again. Chandhok later joked about how his team had let him get a timed lap in early, sort of making up for the decision to not let him race on Sunday. Of course that still rankles in him somewhere but 'will find solace in a commentary box', he said.

When the big boys took to the track, the times tumbled like anything, setting at the end of the day in the 1:24s and 1:25s. Though one thing was very clear, they all loved the flowing track. Ferrari had a mixed day and it will interesting to see where they finish in qualifying and indeed if they have race pace on Sunday, like they magically discover. Toro Rosso looked good again after Korea and might just give Mercedes GP a couple of sleepless nights.

The buzz of the day was Bernie Ecclestone. The F1 supremo celebrated his 81st birthday and showed no signs of slowing down still. He was up and about the paddock, greeting the VIPs and taking care of business as usual.

There were two media tours in the day. The first was in the Red Bull garage, where we were shown the area where the cars were being worked on by the mechanics after the first practice. I asked, among other things, about team morale, when one of the drivers questions his team's motives in favour of the other driver. The question was sidestepped with a smile and a simple answer, 'we work for both drivers equally here at Red Bull.' Well, not for nothing has a beverages' company climbed so high in the F1 charts. The other visit in the afternoon was to the Ferrari garage.

Later in the evening, at the press conference, Vijay Mallya stressed on the need for Force India to do well here, again. He asked for nothing less than a 110 percent from his drivers and his team, and he was serious about it. 'Dream come true' he had exclaimed!

The day ended with a small conversation with Anthony Hamilton, Lewis' father, and now manager of Paul Di Resta. He had a very interesting point to make about his involvement with Force India's 'One from a Billion' initiative, where they are looking to harness young Indian drivers' potential for F1.

It was a thought that rankled long after the chat had ended. Surely, when the time comes, an Indian driver could indeed be running for pole here at his home Grand Prix. It is a pipe dream, not just for Mallya or Chandhok or Karthikeyan, but for all Indians who will be here over the next two days.

And what is the harm in dreaming? It has got us here to the inaugural Indian GP. It will take us into the future as well, hopefully.

Day Three: Saturday, 29 October

No dogs or bats; this time, the day was all about V8 powered cars crying out in pure fury. On Saturday, the Indian Grand Prix got a taste of what qualifying tastes like. And the crowds, built up through a hazy morning, and went back wanting more.

The tone overall was getting serious as FIA president Jean Todt descended here and went about taking a small tour of the facility. Almost as if the festivities had ceased and Formula One, for once, was showing a poker straight face this weekend.

First, I made way to the back straight where quite a few generator trucks were parked. The poor souls who have worked hard to get the circuit in place were denied entry. I joined them on the roof of the truck carriers and found out that clicking a picture of a F1 car isn't an easy job. I tried changing my position and thought the exit of the pit-lane would be an ideal place. From there, the viewing angle was wider; one could see the first corner as well as the change in elevation unto the tight third corner. I stood there for forty minutes and despite wearing ear plugs, my ear drums took quite some punishment. The other observation pertained to how late Red Bull cars brake as compared to other cars. Going into the first corner, both Sebastian Vettel and Mark Webber were braking only after crossing the 50 metre marker, thanks to the awesome levels of downforce they can generate. Alternately, all other cars, including McLaren, braked earlier. Adrian Newey is truly a master at designing his cars!

Post that session, I had the opportunity to talk to Nico Hulkenberg. And that is what he wants to be doing, driving on Sundays and not Fridays. Force India has been a good experience for him, given that he is a reserve and test driver, and there isn't much in-season testing now. So he is pleased with the driving time he has been afforded. However, he is a little impatient about the driver line-up announcement that team boss Vijay Mallya wants to make only in December. Meanwhile, he still has fond memories of his time spent with Rubens Barrichello at Williams.

Qualifying began with BBC's Jake Humphrey and Eddie Jordan, later joined by Rowan Atkinson (Mr Bean). Vettel had been quickest in third practice, so there was no reason to not expect him to take yet another pole position, his 13th of the season. There were surprises in store before we got to Q3 though. Jenson Button had spoken about winning this race, but he complained early about lack of rear-end grip. Michael Schumacher had a torrid time, blocked by homeboy Narain Karthikeyan, who will be serving a five-place grid penalty for that offence.

Local race fans turn out for the inaugural Indian Formula One Grand Prix at the Buddh International Circuit

Schumacher and Button did get into Q2 late, using soft tyres, and they wouldn't like that from a strategy point of view. The 2009 champion moved on to Q3, but the seven time champion and crowd favourite had to make do with 12th. He moved up to 11th as Vitaly Petrov served his five-place penalty from Friday. At the head of the order, it was about Vettel and his only real challenger, Lewis Hamilton. In the end, the reigning double world champion made it look easy again, almost 0.3 seconds clear at the front. Hamilton was happy to move to fifth because of his penalty, as he thinks there is a chance to get on the podium. Fernando Alonso is chasing a podium as always, and Felipe Massa had a crash late in the day – taking extra kerb and breaking his right suspension. But the most interesting quote came from Mark Webber. When asked if he would be okay with Sebastian Vettel helping to get a first win in the season, he replied, 'I don't want any places off Vettel.'

Force India didn't disappoint their fans here. Adrian Sutil will start 8th and didn't run in Q3, so he should be good for the race in terms of soft tyres. I spoke with a member of the team and they are confident of a good result for him and also for Paul Di Resta who will start 12th. Tyres are the key with the softs being nearly two seconds quicker than the hard tyres. And one of the Renault mechanics claimed that some teams might look to do just one lap on the hards. All in all, it would mean a whole lot of pit stops and even more action on track. No dogs or bats; this time, the day was all about V8 powered cars crying out in pure fury. On Saturday, the Indian Grand Prix got a taste of what qualifying tastes like. And the crowds, built up through a hazy morning, and went back wanting more.

The tone overall was getting serious as FIA president Jean Todt descended here and went about taking a small tour of the facility. All prominent BBC commentators came, and there was a working atmosphere all around. Almost as if the festivities had ceased and Formula One, for once, was showing a poker straight face this weekend.

First, I made way to the back straight where quite a few generator trucks were parked. The poor souls who have worked hard to get the circuit in place were denied entry. I joined them on the roof of the truck carriers and found out that clicking a picture of a F1 car isn't an easy job. Half the time, all you catch is an empty snap, with only the barriers in focus.

I tried changing my position and thought the exit of the pit-lane would be an ideal place. From there, the viewing angle was wider; one could see the first corner as well as the change in elevation unto the tight third corner. The other observation pertained to how late Red Bull cars brake as compared to other cars. Going into the first corner, both Sebastian Vettel and Mark Webber were braking only after crossing the 50 metre marker, thanks to the awesome levels of downforce they can generate. Alternately, all other cars, including McLaren, braked earlier. Adrian Newey is truly a master at designing his cars!

Post that session, I had the opportunity to talk to Nico Hulkenberg. Force India has been a good experience for him, given that he is a reserve and test driver, and there isn't much in-season testing now. So he is pleased with the driving time he has been afforded. However, he is a little impatient about the driver line-up announce-

Celebrity turnout at the F1 (clockwise from above left): Sachin Tendulkar, Deepika Padukone and Siddharth Mallya, Robert Vadra, Vijay Mallya with Lara Dutta, Sameera Reddy, Shilpa,and sister Shamita Shetty,, Harbhajan Singh, and Rowan Atkinson

Grand Prix grid girls on the track during the drivers' parade in the Formula One Indian Grand Prix

ment that team boss Vijay Mallya wants to make only in December. Meanwhile, he still has fond memories of his time spent with Rubens Barrichello at Williams, though he is sad about how it ended. 'They told me quite late that I won't be driving for them, so that wasn't very good.'

Qualifying began with BBC's Jake Humphrey and Eddie Jordan, later joined by Rowan Atkinson (Mr Bean). Vettel had been quickest in third practice, so there was no reason to not expect him to take yet another pole position, his 13th of the season. There were surprises in store before we got to Q3 though. Jenson Button had spoken about winning this race, but he complained early about lack of rear-end grip. Michael Schumacher had a torrid time, blocked by homeboy Narain Karthikeyan, who will be serving a five-place grid penalty for that offence.

Schumacher and Button did get into Q2 late, using soft tyres, and they wouldn't like that from a strategy point of view. The 2009 champion moved on to Q3, but the seven time champion and crowd favourite had to make do with 12th. He moved up to 11th as Vitaly Petrov served his five-place penalty from Friday. At the head of the order, it was about Vettel and his only real challenger, Lewis Hamilton. In the end, the reigning double world champion made it look easy again, almost 0.3 seconds clear at the front. Adrian Sutil will start 8th and didn't run in Q3, so he should be good for the race in terms of soft tyres. I spoke with a member of the team and they are confident of a good result for him and also for Paul Di Resta who will start 12th. Tyres are the key with the softs being nearly two seconds quicker than the hard tyres. And one of the Renault mechanics claimed that some teams might look to do just one lap on the hards. All in all, it would mean a whole lot of pit stops and even more action on track.

Day Four: Sunday, 30 October

95000. That was the attendance at the inaugural Indian Grand Prix. After a couple of decades in the making, almost two years to develop a facility from scratch and many months of headaches for organizers over various issues, the race finally happened on Sunday. The morning was a little less hazy than Saturday, and as per reports, nearly 60,000 cars were headed for the Buddh International Circuit. Nearly a thousand people were there, a very unusual number for the start of any race on the calendar. The paddock had been abuzz since work began in earnest, as Indian celebrities made a beeline for the inaugural event.

The race was a bit dull, never mind the first time experience it provided to innumerable souls. There had been a lot of talk of overtaking, but dust off the racing line meant the drivers were a bit wary about it. Most obviously, the DRS was going to help them on the long back straight, but almost everyone agreed that turns 9 through 12 were the most special part of the track. They are in a parabolic shape, almost resembling Curva Parabolica at Monza (Italy), yet giving the Indian Grand Prix an identity of its own.

The crowd though would certainly feel disappointed with Force India. There had been a lot of noise from them about doing well in this race, and even talked about being aggressive on the strategy. But both Adrian Sutil and Paul Di Resta went backwards in the race, the former just about finishing in points. Speaking to Vijay Mallya afterwards wasn't easy. 'It wasn't at all a bad result for us. We are proud of having achieved what we have. And will do better in Abu Dhabi', he said.

Felipe Massa made sure that the media centre was entertained enough. One isn't sure how many of the watching crowd know their history but the journalists gathered here were cheering and clapping when the two of them collided on lap 24. One assumes that is part of the circus, the scribes getting something juicier to write. And it happens in every sport.

Lewis looked a bit forlorn after the race though, and apologized to his team. A point to which McLaren team boss, Martin Whitmarsh took kindly, 'I have told him many times he has nothing to say sorry for, he is a racing driver. You make mistakes, learn from them and move on', he told gathered journalists. Massa didn't agree to his blame in their latest affair and it is interesting to note that for a racing driver, how tough it is to do that. When Jenson Button (second place for McLaren) on his way to the podium was told by Fernando Alonso (third place for Ferrari) about their clash, he said, 'Oh Jesus'!

Sebastian Vettel won his eleventh race of the season and he really wanted to win this one. He got pole, led all the laps, got the fastest lap, and won the race, again; is there any stopping his dominance? The reigning double world champion rated this win highly and it can be judged from one of his comments later on, 'India is a big country with a lot of people, but they are happy and they enjoy life. At the end of your life, its friendships, emotions and thoughts that you take away with you, rather than what's in your bank balance. So, even though people don't have a lot here, they are a lot richer in many and we can learn from that.' At the other end of the spectrum was Narain Karthikeyan. Another wonder that finishing 17th can also make a racing driver this happy. But that happens when it is your home race, when you didn't think one is going to happen in your career. 'It is the best I could have wished for, beating my teammate and one Lotus car too. It is an awesome feeling to have completed the first ever Indian Grand Prix', he said.

As fans and spectators, we have experienced something different from what we have known all this while, and we like it.

Red Bull-Renault driver Sebastian Vettel (C), McLaren-Mercedes driver Jenson Button of Britain (R), and Ferrari driver Fernando Alonso (L), after winning the Airtel Formula One Indian Grand Prix 2011

'A Formula One car is something special and to be one of the few people in the world to drive one feels pretty cool.'

He first made a name for himself in India when he won the Formula Maruti championship - one of relatively few junior series running in his home country. He quickly progressed to the Asia-wide Formula 2000 series and won that too. In 2002 he pitted his talents against the ultra-competitive British Formula 3 field, and in his second year in the championship he finished a very respectable third with seven victories. Alongside his British F3 campaigns, he competed in a handful of races in the Worldseries by Renault and in 2005 drove three races for his country in A1 GP. In 2006 he returned to Asia to drive in the less competitive Formula V6 championship, which he duly won. That opened the door to GP2 the next year, where he steadily progressed and took a victory in the sprint race at Spa Francorchamps. His promising start in GP2 secured him two days of testing for Red Bull, at which he held his own against a whole field of both established F1 drivers and young hopefuls.

For 2008 he was paired with Bruno Senna at the race-winning i-Sport outfit in GP2 and was a consistent points' scorer. However, as he scrapped for top-eight finishes and a single win, Senna was challenging for the championship and finished the season with over double Chandhok's points. In 2009 he stayed in GP2, but his season was dogged by retirements and bad luck, and he finished a lowly 18th in the standings.

With sponsors' money and his potentially lucrative nationality as negotiating tools, he became a serious contender for a F1 race seat in 2010. His dream finally came true just a week before the start of the season when he was announced as a race driver for HRT alongside his old sparring partner Senna. His amiable personality won him a legion of fans in the junior series and his popularity continued to grow in his debut year. However, his budget didn't match that of Japanese Sakon Yamamoto and after the British Grand Prix, he was left without a drive for the rest of the season.

After leaving HRT his future in the sport was far from certain, but he was picked up by Lotus as a third driver, going on to race in the 2011 German Grand Prix in place of Jarno Trulli as the team entertain the idea of an Indian driver participating in the inaugural Indian Grand Prix. Despite a less than convincing performance, he is still, by far, the best-qualified Indian for F1, and his winning personality has earned him respect up and down the paddock.

Karun Chandhok during the Formula One Indian Grand Prix at Buddh International Circuit

Q&A with KARUN CHANDOK

Karun, I want to start with your affinity to motorsports. Did it begin early for you? Or were you drawn to some other sports as well?

Ever since I was a kid, all I can ever remember being really interested is race cars. I used to watch F1 races since the age of 2, even though it never came on TV at that time. We used to get videos of the races from friends in the UK and I loved watching it again and again even though they were replays. I always knew I wanted to be a racing driver, but I had to work hard to make it happen. When I was finishing school I was 96kgs and was told if I wanted to race, I had to lose weight in order to first fit in the car. So I lost 26 kgs in less than six months and went on to win the Indian National Racing Championship.

In India, parents give due importance to studies and pursuing a career in sports, least of all motorsports which was even less popular in India when you started out, doesn't leave much space for that. So how did your family support your decision to go racing?

This would not have been possible without the support of my parents. It is hard to explain what they have sacrificed to help me get here, but simply put this would have not been possible without them. My father used to race and my grandfather before that, so it was a natural progression for me to get into racing. I have always been a big racing fan and used to accompany my father to the race track every day. He has definitely been a big influence for me and more importantly supported me throughout my career, through the ups and downs. He has let me make my own decisions and supported me through every step of the way. Quite honestly, without my parents this would have never been possible.

It's true that today Motorsport isn't yet seen as a career option in India, but I am hoping to change this and work with manufacturers and sponsors in the future to set up affordable structures for the future generations to make progress.

You have been racing for a long time now, beginning with junior events before moving onto bigger series such as Formula Asia, and then gradually working your way to the European scene. How necessary is this stage for a racer, and what was your learning from this period? Any favourite memories?

It is a necessity for all aspiring drivers to work their way up the ladder to reach Formula One. Sadly, there is no shortcut or easy way up. Every driver on the grid today has worked their way up through junior categories to finally reach here. For any driver to be successful in motorsports, it's important to be successful in Europe, there is no doubt about it. Hence, I believe that it is really important to have a genuinely competitive junior single-seater series in the region that can feed Asian drivers into Europe.

Winning my first Formula Asia race in 2001 in the Philippines was special as it was my first International win, and then winning at Spa in GP2 in 2007 was fantastic as well.

When Narain Karthikeyan first raced in Formula One in 2005, it must have uplifted your spirits as well. You were his team-mate in the World Series by Nissan in 2004. What were your thoughts on an Indian finally making to the F1 grid and how did it fuel your ambition further?

For me, the most important thing was to have self-belief and belief in the fact that I belonged in Europe and competed hard against the best drivers in the world. Narain getting into F1 was obviously great for him and India, but to be honest, it had no real impact on me or my career.

Soon after, you moved to the GP2 series, which is a stepping stone for getting into Formula One, as the past has shown us. Having raced in F1 thereafter, what is the obvious difference between the two, and in hindsight, how well prepared were you for F1 having raced here?

The move to GP2 series was big for me and my performance there did wonders for my confidence. My first win in Spa, in a car which was definitely not the best on the grid showed me that there was more to come. To hear our national anthem for the first time in a Formula One race weekend is something that motivates you to want more and more. GP2 is the best stepping stone to F1. The cars are quick – the closest thing to F1 in the world, we race at the same circuits on the same day as F1 so there are a lot of big plus points there. The biggest differences are actually outside the car where you have to work with a huge amount of engineers and people in marketing and PR as well, which puts a lot of pressure on your time.

How was racing with Ayrton Senna's nephew, your team-mate at iSport and then later at HRT, Bruno?

Bruno and I get along very well and we are really good friends off the track as well, which is not very common in this sport. Even today, despite us being with different teams we keep speak regularly and catch up away from the track. A lot of people had told me it would be hard working with him and his family and the rest of it, but that is not the case at all. His mum and sisters are great people and I have ended up being an honorary member of their family !

At both iSport and HRT we had a great working relationship with the engineers and the team members. We always had a similar style and similar requirements from the car which is good for the engineers to carry out parallel programs. I think because you are friends, you trust each other a bit more.

Now about the big moment. Can you tell us how the F1 break happened for you?

Getting into F1 with Hispania was definitely a huge step for me. At the end of 2009, we had some options to be test driver with other teams up and down the pitlane. So the options were: be a test driver and do two or three days of testing a year; we could have gone back to GP2. We had plenty of options on the table, but I felt ready to do F1. I was quite optimistic that something would happen in F1, but both my dad and

I were clear in our minds that if we had to make the break, then 2010 was our best chance because there were new seats available.

We started talking to Adrian Campos (previous owner of HRT) since Valencia 2009, but things were dragging on for various reasons. We started to look at other options and were close to other deals, but nothing materialized. Then Colin (Kolles) called to say he was going to be taking over the running of the team. We were able to work very quickly with him and, along with Mr. Bernie Ecclestone's advice, sorted out a deal.

F1 enthusiasts in India were a little disappointed that HRT could not provide a better car and that your season ended prematurely. Amidst all the negativity, what positives did you take from 2010?

For me personally, I only saw the positives. I fulfilled a lifelong ambition of being a Formula One driver. I proved to the whole world that I belonged there, even though the car was not the best. I managed to be the highest finisher for the team out of the 4 drivers they had. Other teams took notice of me and were impressed with what I had to offer. Drivers like Alonso, Webber, Trulli etc. have all started at the back of the grid and worked their way up the grid, and I plan to do the same. I will always be grateful to HRT as they gave me my big break into Formula One. The season was a lot better than I expected as I finished 14th twice to put the team ahead of Virgin Racing in the overall standings. I finished 8 out of the 10 races that I drove in with no real mistakes which was our aim all along

Karun Chandhok's performance at the FIA Formula One World Championship 2011 in Germany

and earned the respect of the people in the paddock, and the highly critical F1 specialist media.

Now you are biding your time at Lotus. You have raced in Germany already and have many test sessions coming your way. How different is it from the HRT experience? When can we expect an announcement as a full-time racing driver for Lotus? Will we see you drive at the inaugural Indian Grand Prix?

I am very grateful to Tony Fernandes and Team Lotus for giving me an opportunity to drive in Germany. One of the main reasons I came here was because I actually believe that I will get more in the medium-long term from Lotus than anywhere else. The objective is not to be a permanent third driver, the objective is to be back racing. The team has made tremendous progress over the last 18 months, more than the other two new teams, so from that point of view, it's interesting. But any racing driver wants to race and I am no different. The team has some great people with Tony (Fernandes), Mike (Gascoyne), Riad (Asmat), and Mark (Smith) etc. At the end of the day it is important to be a team member as everyone is doing their part. For me it would be a dream come true to drive at the Indian Grand Prix, but unfortunately, it is not in my hands. I would like to be back racing full time and not only at the Indian GP, and that is my aim for the future.

Being an Indian F1 driver, there are obvious connects with Force India. Yet no such move has happened although there has been a lot of talk, both positive and negative. Your comments on the same?

There is actually not much to say. My ambition has always been to be an F1 driver and I have that opportunity with Team Lotus, and I am very happy with it.

Dr Vijay Mallya has said that currently no Indian driver is good enough for driving in F1/his team. Do you think that is a negative comment in light of the efforts and sacrifices you have made to get to the highest level of motorsport? Also, how tough is it to maintain your position in the sport, coming from a culture that is only just growing into F1 and motorsport?

I have made my comments with regard to this very clear in the past, and it is a closed chapter for me now.

In sport, any sport, I think to a large extent, people within the sport look beyond colour, race, or nationality. In the eyes of the media and the fans, I will always be an Indian and I'm very proud of that but for the people within the teams, they don't really care where you come from!

Do you feel that Indian fans currently lack an understanding of F1, especially when they are so easily turned off by seeing their drivers at the back of the grid? Is that also a reason why sponsors tend to withdraw support mid-way through the season, leaving drivers in the lurch? Do you think Indian drivers need better backing?

I think motorsport, and F1 in particular has grown leaps and bounds over the last decade. We have two drivers and our inaugural grand prix coming up, so we are definitely on the map with regard to Formula One. After cricket, F1 is one of the most watched sports in India so the understanding is definitely there.

I do think that today, the fans, by and large, still don't understand that it is the whole package and not only the driver that makes difference in F1 but it's our job as the ambassadors of the sport to educate them and hopefully the media will support us in this process. Sponsorship in the sport has always been an issue, barring some companies. Hopefully , the Grand Prix coming to India will open up the door more sponsor opportunities.

You are quite popular with F1 fans all over as also in the pitlane. Not to mention, your stints as an F1 commentator have been well praised. Comments?

For me, motorsports is a passion, not a job. Driving race cars is the most fantastic experience in the world. I have worked with ESPN Star, BBC, Sky Sports, and Eurosport, and so far everyone seems to be pretty complimentary of my commentary work.

Last but not the least, what is your message to Indian fans ahead of the inaugural Indian GP? How do you see motorsport and F1 rising in India in the near future?

With the Indian GP happening later this year, the motorsport brand in India is going to grow rapidly. The domestic racing scene in India has evolved a great deal.

With the Indian GP happening this year, I hope the sport's popularity is going to grow rapidly and this way, more people will want to be associated with the sport. I am talking about corporates, universities, fans, and consumers etc. Our biggest challenge as drivers has always been funding, so I now hope that more corporates step forward and see the benefits in being associated with the sport.

BUDDH INTERNATIONAL CIRCUIT

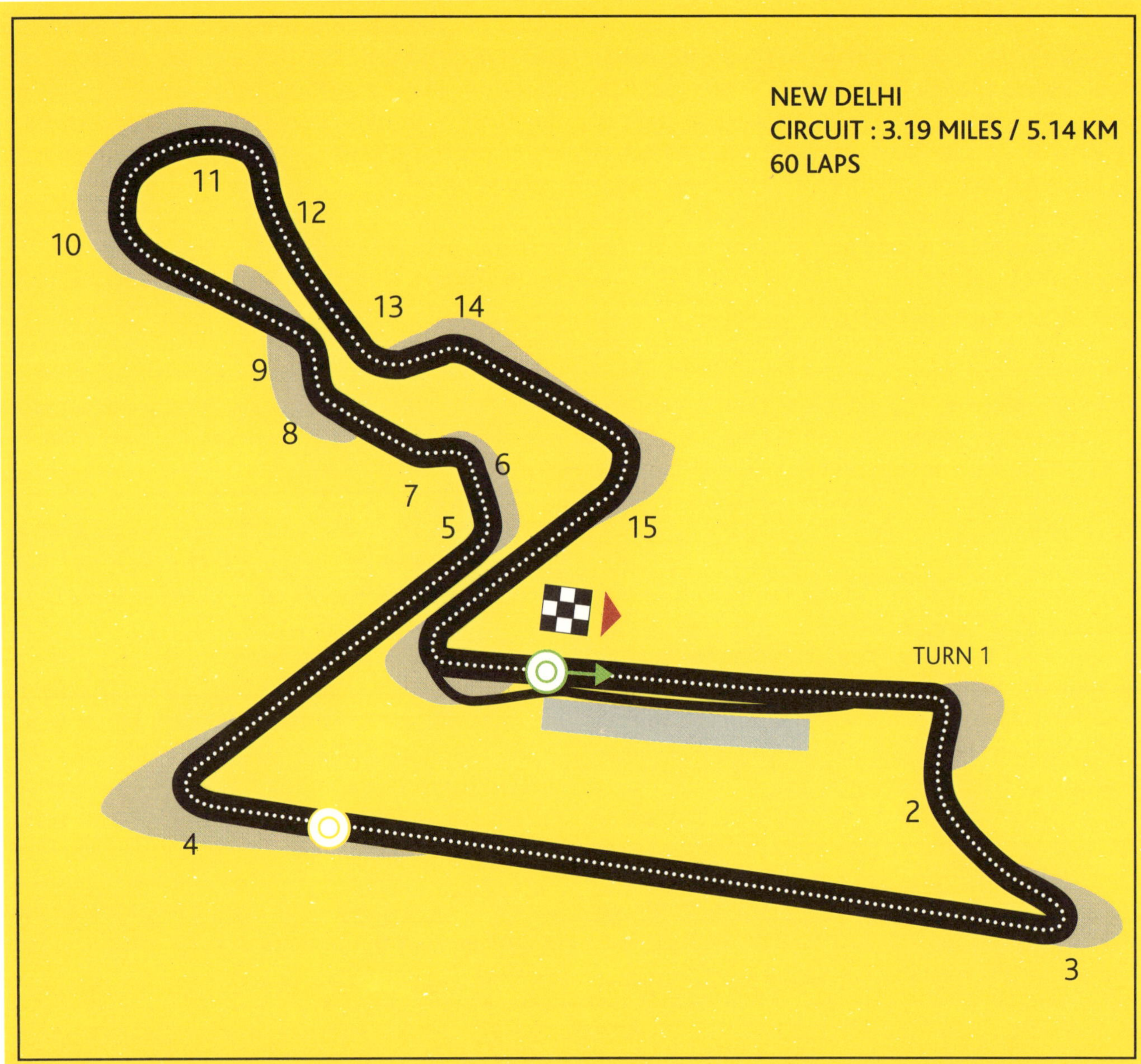

The 5.14 km long Buddh International Race Circuit has been designed by renowned German architect and race-track designer, Herman Tilke, who has also designed other world class race circuits in Malaysia, Bahrain, China, Turkey, Indonesia, the UAE, South Africa, South Korea, and the US.

The circuit will be part of the 2,500 acres Jaypee Greens Sports City, which is planned to include a 100,000 seat cricket stadium, 18-hole golf course, 25000-seat hockey stadium and a sports academy. The sports complex is expected to cost $40 billion and generate $170m of revenue annually, and employ 10,000 people. Four million cubic tons of earth was moved to give the track plenty of undulation, and it rises 14 metres between Turns One and Three alone. Inspiration has also been drawn from rival venues' best features, with Turkey's infamous Turn Eight inspiring a double-apex corner, slightly banked, which forms part of a 'mini-arena' which alone will accommodate 13,000 spectators. The expected lap time for a Formula One car around the track is 1 minute 27.02 seconds, at an average speed of 210.03 km/h (131 mph). At the end of the long straight between corners 3 and 4, Formula One cars are expected to reach a top speed of about 318 km/h (198 mph).

In an interesting move, organizers also consulted several of the Formula One teams before construction began in earnest. The track design was run in various factory simulators and as a result several amendments were made in an effort to boost overtaking for the drivers – and excitement for the fans.

The start-finish straight is flanked on both sides, by the pit-lane and by the majestic grand stand as has come to be the norm across the world. Accelerating through to Turn One, the drivers will then be hard on the brakes as they look to make places at the start. Turn Three then has a blind apex but the circuit here is wide enough for the drivers to take different lines going into the straight and setting themselves up for overtaking opportunities. In these three turns alone, the track elevation changes by 104 metres.

Over one kilometre in length, the back-straight will see speeds in excess of 300 km/h. Again, at the end of the straight, drivers will have to go hard on the brakes and create chances for overtaking, going into the sweeping right hander. A quick accelerating exit takes the cars towards a flowing Turn Five, and a series of fast left-right bends take them towards Turn Ten and Eleven. It is a hugely fast double apex corner, somewhat similar to the Turn Eight at Istanbul Park Circuit (Turkey), with cars making their way through at more than 220 km/h. The only difference with that Turkish circuit is that there is a huge grandstand in place here, giving 13000 spectators a splendid view of the action!

Through Turns Thirteen, Fourteen, and Fifteen, there are more elevation changes, as the final turn leads off sharply into the pit-lane or across the finish line.

Nico Rosberg at the Formula One, Buddh International Circuit, Greater Noida, GP 2011

LG LG

airtel
airtel
airtel
UBS
LG
airtel
airtel
airtel
LG
airtel
airtel
airtel
LG

In the present scenario, Force India has only been competing in the F1 championship since 2008, after the teams' name change was sanctioned by the FIA, but the origins of the team go back to 1991.

The team was formed from what was originally known as Jordan Grand Prix, which had been active in the championship since 1991. Owner Eddie Jordan put the team up for sale and they were bought by the Midland group in 2005, and renamed Midland F1 Racing. After just a year the team was sold to the Spyker car company near the end of the 2006 season. However, financial restraints saw the team being offered for sale yet again; just a year after Spyker took control. The price was EUR 88 million, much more than was originally paid, and this time it fell into the hands of Orange India Holdings group, with billionaire Indian business man, Vijay Mallya and existing board member Michiel Mol taking over.

Apart from the name and colour scheme, little changed for the 2008 season; Colin Kolles remained principal, Michiel Mol director of F1 racing, and Mike Gascoyne chief technology officer. The team failed to achieve any notable results or score any championship points; Adrian Sutil came closest, holding forth position at the Monaco Grand Prix, until he was rear-ended by Kimi Raikkonen forcing him to retire just ten minutes before the end of the race.

Before the start of the 2009 season, there was a management shake-up which saw Mallya take the role of team principal. The team also signed a deal to use Mercedes engines. However, this did little to improve their

Force India team boss Vijay Mallya and Giancarlo Fisichella celebrate their first podium finish at the Belgian GP, 2009

fortunes, and by race 10 of the season, the team had still yet to score a championship point.

Their fortunes changed in Belgium when Giancarlo Fisichella finally scored points for the team - in impressive fashion he finished second on the podium, bagging eight points for the team. Not to be outdone, Sutil followed this up with a fourth place in Italy to add another five points to the tally. With a total of 13 points, Force India finished second to last in the constructors' championship ahead of Toro Rosso. Their challenge for 2010 is to continue the impressive form they showed at the end of the 2009 season, and challenge for more point and podium finishes.

The season began with points in Bahrain, with Liuzzi finishing at ninth position. Sutil had qualified in tenth, but was involved in a first-lap incident with the Renault of Robert Kubica. He ultimately recovered to finish in twelfth position. In Australia, Sutil again qualified in the top ten, with Liuzzi qualifying thirteenth. Liuzzi finished the race in seventh, while Sutil retired with an engine problem. In Malaysia Sutil scored ten points with fifth and Liuzzi retired early due to a throttle problem, his first retirement of the season. In the next few races, apart from a retirement from Liuzzi, the Force Indias had quiet races in the midfield, staying mainly out of the action in front of and behind them, with Sutil scoring points in Spain. At Monaco both cars finished the race in eighth and ninth, avoiding the numerous incidents, giving the team their first double points finish. In Turkey, Sutil finished 9th scoring two points, while Liuzzi finished 13th. At the following race in Montreal, both cars finished in the points with Liuzzi finishing 9th and Sutil, 10th.

In January 2011, the team announced that reserve driver Paul di Resta would be promoted to a race seat for the season to partner Adrian Sutil, while Nico Hulkenberg would be reserve driver.

Adrian Sutil has been quite consistent for Force India

Is this Indian Grand Prix race weekend your first time in India?

No. I have been here quite a few times, for promotions and press conferences. I have been to Delhi, Mumbai, and Bangalore in this time, and I am enjoying the reception fans have given us. I enjoy being here; it is a bit different, but you try to soak in as many good things as possible. It is very different from life in Europe. Of course, the best part of this experience is the Buddh International Circuit, and I love the facility. They have done a very good job of building this track.

How has your time spent with Sahara Force India this season been?

I would say it has been a very promising season. Honestly, I am not in the role which I want to be in, as test and reserve driving duties don't always give you the best opportunity. But whatever chances I have got to drive the car, Friday morning practice sessions, the entire team has worked really hard with me. They have made me very comfortable here and I want to thank them for giving me so many Friday sessions, because normally, reserve drivers are not given so many sessions. It has given me a chance to showcase to them what I am capable of. I am pretty happy at this team and going forward, Sahara Force India has a lot of potential.

There is a lack of testing in Formula One now, so in that light, how important does your role become in the team?

Very important, because without that Friday running, I wouldn't be the driver I am now. If one of the two drivers is not able to race for whatever reasons, I would be able

Force India drivers, Adrian Sutil and Nico Hulkenberg at a publicity event during the Indian GP

to straight away jump into the car and drive, and perform at the top of my level. They have kept me sharp, kept me going, have learnt how to use DRS and KERS, and honestly, if I hadn't done those sessions, I would be totally a different driver now. And then you can lose your Formula One status very quickly, so yes, I am thankful for these sessions that have kept me in the game.

There has been a lot of talk about you driving for Sahara Force India in 2012, replacing Adrian Sutil. What do you have to say to that?

As always, there is a lot of speculation going on in the Formula One paddock. I have read about it in newspapers and websites as well. But I have to go by what Vijay (Mallya) says, and he has said that he will make a decision in a couple of weeks' time.

You were with Williams in 2010 and they have a good pedigree. They have been champions in the past, even though they are a middle rung team now. But it was your debut year in F1 with them. So how was the experience racing for them?

You know the first year of Formula One is very special, always, for everyone. I have a lot of great memories with them, and obviously, the pole position in Brazil stands out. We had some very good weekends apart from that, such as Monza. Korea started well, but we had a puncture, so that affected our race two laps from the end. I had a very good relationship with all the mechanics and engineers there. But it didn't end too well there for me. They told me very late in the day that I won't be driving for them in 2011 and that wasn't very nice of them.

Rubens Barrichello was your team-mate there and he is the most experienced driver in F1 today. Did you enjoy pairing up with him?

I enjoyed working with Rubens a lot, and as you said, he is the most experienced driver on the grid, so I learnt a lot from him. During the course of last season, I realized how good he was and I miss being his team-mate.

Can you talk about that pole position lap in Brazil last year?

I think it was the perfect lap for the sort of conditions we had then. It had stopped raining and the track was drying up very fast, so it was a bit of dry and wet both. And the car was feeling just great in those conditions, perfect set-up and new soft (dry) tyres with optimum pressure in them, which is very crucial on a partly dry-partly wet circuit. So when they put on the slicks, I was very aggressive, trying to get as much heat into the tyres as possible. And my lap times kept improving as I got more and more heat into them. It is quite tricky to get the braking point right in those conditions and also to stay on the dry line, but that was the perfect lap and it was quite sensational in the end, yeah! It was an emotional moment for me, my first ever pole position.

How different is driving in Formula One than in junior Formulae? How different is your preparation and concentration?

Formula One is the pinnacle of motorsport and it is very special to be part of this racing series. Of course it is the quite a challenge and difficult to get set in here. But then you have the junior Formulae, Formula BMW, Formula Renault, you name the series. These racing series prepare you for the challenges ahead, for Formula One if you get there eventually. I had some mega seasons in Formula Three and GP2 as well which prepared me and taught me lot of stuff that ultimately brought me to F1.

There are quite a few German drivers in Formula One at the moment, six to be precise. Top of the ladder are Michael Schumacher who is an all time great and Sebastian Vettel is now reigning double world champion. So what sort of impact are you looking to make in F1?

I have just done one year of racing in Formula One so the main aim is to establish myself here over the next three to four years. I hope I can do many more years in F1 than that because I love this sport. I love the way people work here, very professional and driving these cars is a very big privilege. So I just want to stay here and in terms of what I want to achieve, of course I want to be successful. I want to win races; and in the short term, I want to be racing again next year and take it from there.

Coming back to Sahara Force India then, Vijay Mallya leads your team and you have quite a few Indians in the team as well, taking care of various functions. You have the Indian Grand Prix happening now. So, how Indian is this team?

See, the team is based in England and they have to be there. Because there is the whole motorsport culture in Europe and you just cannot go away from there. Formula One is only just coming to India. So any F1 team would think hard before setting up base away from Europe. Having said that, Vijay is an Indian and now you have Sahara coming in to the team. We have a lot of Indian people doing marketing and communications for the team.

And finally, ahead of the inaugural Indian Grand Prix, what message would you want to give to F1 fans here?

I hope we can get their attention by doing a good race weekend here. I am sure after this weekend hopefully people here will know a bit more about Formula One and hopefully they support this sport more and more, especially our team which is an Indian team. And hopefully we will be able to pay them back by bringing in some nice results get the team a closer feel of 'Indian'.

NARAIN KARTHIKEYAN

'I am not interested in driving for Force India.'

His father being a former Indian national rally champion, winning fuelled his ambition of becoming India's first Formula One driver. He raced first in 1992 in Formula Maruti, and made good on his scholarship to become a semi-finalist in the Pilote Elf Competition for Formula Renault cars. He returned to India to race in Formula Maruti for the 1993 season, and in the same year, he also competed in the Formula Vauxhall Junior championship in Great Britain. In 1994, he returned to the UK, racing in the Formula Ford Zetec series, as the number two works Vector driver for the Foundation Racing team.

In 1995, Karthikeyan graduated to the Formula Asia Championship for just four races. In 1996, he had a full season in the series and became the first Indian and the first Asian to win the Formula Asia International series. He moved back to Britain in 1997, to compete in the British Formula Opel Championship with the Nemesis Motorsport team, taking a pole position and win at Donington Park and finishing sixth in the overall points standings. In 1998, Karthikeyan made his debut in the British Formula Three Championship with the Carlin Motorsport team. Competing in only 10 rounds, he managed two third place finishes in the final two races of the season, at Spa-Francorchamps and Silverstone, to finish 12th overall. He continued in the championship for 1999, finishing on the podium five times, including two wins at Brands Hatch. Continuing his drive in the British F3 Championship in 2000, he finished fourth overall in the standings, and also took pole position and fastest laps in the Macau Grand Prix.

HRT cosworth driver Narain Karthikeyan waves to the crowd during the practice session of Formula One's Indian Grand Prix

Karthikeyan started 2001 in the Formula Nippon F3000 Championship, finishing the year amongst the top ten. In the same year, he became the first Indian to ever drive a Formula One car, testing for the Jaguar Racing team at Silverstone on 14 June. Impressed with his performance, he was then offered a test drive in the Jordan-Honda EJ11 at Silverstone in September. Karthikeyan again tested for Jordan, at Mugello in Italy in October, finishing just half a second of the pace off Jordan's lead driver, Jean Alesi.

In 2002, he moved into the Telefonica World Series with Team Tata RC Motorsport, taking a pole position and setting the fastest non-Formula One lap time at the Interlagos Circuit in Brazil. Continuing in the renamed Superfund Word Series in 2003, Karthikeyan won two races and took three other podium positions on his way to fourth overall in the championship. These results earned him another Formula One test drive, this time with the Minardi team. He was offered a race drive for the 2004 season, but was unable to raise the necessary sponsorship funds to seal the deal.

On 1 February 2005, Karthikeyan announced that he had signed the preliminary deal with Jordan Formula One team and said that he would be their main driver for the 2005 Formula One season, thus making him India's first Formula One racing driver. He achieved his first points in the 2005 United States Grand Prix under farcical circumstances, as all but three teams pulled out due to an argument over tyre safety. Karthikeyan finished fourth, finishing ahead of the two Minardi drivers but behind team mate Monteiro. Apart from the USGP, Karthikeyan's highest finish was 11th place. Because the Jordan team was taken over and renamed Midland for the 2006 season, the management change prompted some doubt over Karthikeyan's future at the team. Near the end of 2005, Karthikeyan announced he would not be driving for Midland the following year allegedly due to their demand that he pay as much as $11.7 million to secure his seat on the team. Karthikeyan tested for Williams at Spain and finished a respectable fifth, outpacing the confirmed Williams second driver, Nico Rosberg. On 27 January 2006, Williams confirmed Karthikeyan as their fourth driver.

On 6 January 2011, Karthikeyan announced that he would drive for the Hispania team in the 2011 season, following five years away from active involvement in the championship. However after a not so successful first half of the season, he was replaced by Daniel Ricciardo for the remaining races of the season except the Indian Grand Prix.

Q&A with NARAIN KARTHIKEYAN

Narain, you were close to motorsports from childhood itself. How did it help shape your ambition to race and indeed become a Formula One driver?

Well, I was always attracted to this world of motorsport, primarily because I am from Coimbatore and that is the motorsport hub of India. My family has been associated with racing as well, so it had a huge influence on me, obviously. My father was a rally driver and some of my other relatives have raced too, while also being associated with building race cars. So it was natural that I would follow this path.

You have been associated with a lot of junior Formulae, the F3, Formula Nippon-Nissan, Formula Renault, etc. So when you did well there, how did it shape up your confidence that you could go further, possibly even reach Formula One?

It was the most obvious thing to do. If you have to drive internationally and get into bigger things like Formula One, you have to make a move away from India, and these junior Formulae help with that immensely. Europe

Narain Karthikeyan of HRT steers his car during the qualification session at the race track of Buddh International Circuit

airtel
KARTHIKEYAN
22
airtel
SUTIL
airtel
HAMILTON
TATA
HERO
SINGLE ENTRY
SINGLE ENTRY
DL 2C 8170

is the most obvious destination because primarily, that is where all the action is centered. So you have to make an effort to reach out there, search for an opportunity; and I did just that. I won races in Formula Ford, and then Formula Three. I think that was the start of me getting noticed by Formula One teams..

In 2001, you tested for Jaguar. It took another four years to finally break into F1. How agonizing was the wait?
It is very hard you know. Once that didn't work out as I thought it would, I had to refocus and see what I was doing right or wrong. I had to invent new routes to get into Formula One, because the first approach hadn't really worked. A few years later, something new that I had tried clicked, and I was driving for Jordan; and then with Williams as a test driver. Now I am here at HRT and in a way, have laid down a path for the others to see and follow. I had no set trails to follow and it wasn't easy for me. Hopefully it will be easier for others who would want to join this world of racing.

How was your debut year in 2005, with Jordan?
Oh, that was a super experience. The car was in the midfield or there about, and we were using Bridgestone tyres. Michelin had the edge that year because of rule changes, and we couldn't perform up to what was perhaps expected of us. But they are much cherished memories for me.

You went to Williams next as a test driver and spent considerable time in that role. How was that experience?
Williams are a great team, a legendary team. They have won multiple championships in the past, and being associated with them was a great learning. A test driver role isn't always desired, but I was trying to make a mark and thought that was the platform to do so. You can impress in that role as has happened in the past. Alternately, though in my own experience, I realized it is easier to get lost as a test driver. I gave my best but in the end it didn't turn out to be the best move for me. Having said that, I was very happy to have spent time with such a big team!

You almost vanished from the Formula One scene thereafter and experimented with different racing series, A1GP, Indy Racing, Le Mans, NASCAR, etc. But did you always still want to return to Formula One and what kept that fire burning?
Yes, of course. Formula One is the pinnacle of motorsport and I hadn't achieved what I thought I could in my first stint here. I always wanted another shot at it. I won in A1GP and representing my country there was good. It gave me a wonderful opportunity to win races again and continue to be in the spotlight.

After 2005, you are back at this level of racing, but a lot has changed with the rules and the cars. Was it difficult to adapt?
Well, it was a long time ago and there are obvious differences. But I don't recall very minutely what all differences were there. Coming back now, it was a fresh start for me. Formula One unfortunately depends a lot on the car you drive and this is 'the thing' about this sport. Frustrating as it is, you can't really help it and have to accept it.

Now to the Indian Grand Prix and you will be driving here, the first Indian racer to do so. Has the dream come true?
Phenomenal is the word actually. To host a Grand Prix here in India, I think the organizers have done a fantastic job. Personally, I never thought it would happen in my career, but it is happening now. Having driven at Buddh International Circuit on Sunday, 30 October 2011, I am very, very happy.

What expectations do you have from the Indian Grand Prix?
There is a lot of enthusiasm around here and it is really great to see. I think the race will do very well here in India, and Formula One has been given a fabulous reception, so they will keep coming back. Personally, I am not aiming for anything big; just finish the race and hopefully finish it ahead of my team mate, Daniel Ricciardo. We have to try to achieve what the car is capable of and if we do that, I will be very happy and satisfied.

What message do you want to give the fans ahead of this inaugural Indian Grand Prix?
The way they have greeted Formula One is superb. It is going to be a great spectacle for many years to come. I just want them to enjoy and relish it. For me, it is a tremendous thrill to drive in front of my home crowd.

(Narain Karthikeyan finished 17th in the Indian Grand Prix. His HRT team-mate, Daniel Ricciardo, finished 19th.)

Narain Karthikeyan of India and Hispania Racing Team waves to the crowd as he attends the drivers parade before the inaugural Indian Formula One Grand Prix

SPORTHOTEL RESTAURANT

THE PRE-F1 YEARS

BEFORE 1950

Through the last 125 years, there is but one facet of human civilization that has remained truly consistent – the urge to go quick and quicker still. This need for speed finds its roots in the 1890s, witnessing the turn of the century and advent of industrialization, surviving two World Wars, and spurring forward with German domination in technology and supreme Italian craftsmanship of the steering wheel, forming the bedrock of modern day Formula One world championships.

The first ever car race was held in 1894, from Paris to Rouen, on public roads where 21 drivers competed in the event for a 5000 Franc prize. Needless to say, the French then were the first pioneers of motor racing although they lagged behind Britain and Germany in industrialization. Cars in those days were heavy and steered with a lever instead of a steering wheel. The roads were sand or wood tarred; and the tyres used were solid, not pneumatic. Yet this did not deter the formation of Automobile Club de France, which first organised a race in 1896 from Paris to Marseille and back, rally-style. By the next year, there were encouraging signs that cars for racing purposes, could actually be different from those used for public transportation.

At the same time though, safety concerns were largely-creeping up. Unlike today there were no proper circuits built for the races and spectators lining up the roads were sitting ducks in case of a crash. There were infamous incidents during the 1898 Paris-Nice, 1901 Paris-Berlin and 1903 Paris-Bordeaux-Madrid races that pressed the governments of these countries to ban motorsport events. But sooner rather than later, they bowed to pressure from vested interests to allow racing again, provided the roads were sealed off by barriers. This was the start of closed-circuit racing as we know it today.

With the arrival of the 1900s, the British and German motor industry began to take notice, deciding they could not just sit back and watch, Italy and America too joined in, and they all took steps to bring racing to their own soil. And so the first purpose-built racing track was opened at Brooklands in Surrey in 1907. But by the end of the decade, the French had pulled out from motorsport as such and this was a precursor of the times, as Europe was heading into a financial and political crisis leading to the First World War. Meanwhile on the other side of the Atlantic Ocean, racing was booming. It began with the opening of the Indianapolis Motor Speedway, also in 1907, and paved the way for more such closed, oval speedways across the continent.

Starting line-up at the 1912 Indy 500

Previous pages: The starting grid at the German Grand Prix, 1935 at Nürburgring, Germany

The advent of Chicanes at the 1926 British GP, Brooklands

By the time America entered the war a decade later, racing had come to take a more modern form, albeit basic. Circuits were tweaked, winded and twisted, with the car-design emphasis shifting from pure power to manoeuvring and braking. Post war, two important changes took place in the world of racing. Firstly, a distinction was born in the American and European style of racing and pursuit of technology. The Americans started developing cars exclusively for racing on their oval speedways. Meanwhile, European engineers, having gained much know-how from the war years, worked on high revving overhead camshaft engines mated with light-weight chassis. Fiat were the pioneers of this design, and it points directly to the second major change of that era, that is the dominance of European racing by Italy.

The early 1920s were a competitive battleground for Bugatti, Fiat, and Alfa Romeo cars. By 1925, a World Championship for Manufacturers was very much in play and Alfa Romeo were clear winners, thanks to Antonio Ascari's all-out racing style.

However, he was killed during the French Grand Prix that year, and Alfa Romeo pulled out of racing citing financial reasons, as the world stared at another economic crisis. As the Great Depression set in, the European Automobile Championship (also known as the International Grand Prix) was announced in the year 1931. It invited entries without restrictions on weight or engine capacity. Their prime motive was to keep racing alive. Known as Formula Libre, it prevented motorsport from going into stagnation, and instead becoming a hot bed for some of the best drivers showcasing their skills with some fabulous and most technically advanced racing cars yet. This period was witness to some great duels between Achille Varzi and Tazio Nuvolari, the latter were considered one of the greatest racers of all time. He was at the wheel of many great

TRIVIA

The first race cars with mechanics on board

In the first car race in 1894 from Paris to Rouen, drivers were asked to carry mechanics on board. Count de Dion won the race, but did not have a mechanic on board, so he was disqualified. The 80-mile race included a stop-over for lunch.

wins, especially for Alfa Romeo who were the dominant manufacturer of this era. The 1932 Alfa Romeo P3 was a standout car, winning every race it entered. However that was also the year when their domination ended, as owing to interference by the Italian government, they pulled out of motor racing, owing to interference from the government. It led to the birth of a secondary team, one that would carry on racing with older models born at Monza, and this team came to be known as Scuderia Ferrari.

By the mid-1930s, Adolf Hitler began taking keen interest in racing technology and thought of using it as a tool for Nazi propaganda. This marked a shift from Italian to German engineering with Mercedes and Auto Union (present day Audi) coming to the fore. In the few years remaining before the world would again be plunged into war, the two manufacturers competed for honours in every race and championship across Europe. Varzi signed for Auto Union and Nuvolari kept to Ferrari, but Rudolf Caracciola led Mercedes to three successive titles through 1937 to 1939. The Yugoslavian Grand Prix at Belgrade was the last race before hostilities commenced.

Post the Second World War, German domination came to an obvious end and motorsport only rose slowly. Shortage of oil resources was a major factor. However by 1948, things were again looking up as races across Europe commenced again. Nuvolari, now 56, drove a last great race at Parma in Italy, while Varzi was killed during the Swiss Grand Prix. But the coming of one Juan Manuel Fangio from Argentina at the French Grand Prix that year was the most important marker. Soon, the world would wake up to a new order in motor racing.

Tazio Nuvolari (Alfa-Romeo) leads Achille Varzi (Auto Union) at the 1936 Milan GP

Facing page: Starting grid at the 1935 Coppa Acerbo, Pescara (Italy)

TRAGUARDO

F1 CHAMPIONSHIP BEGINS:

1950 - 1956

Formula One began as Formula A, a set of rules to which all participants and cars must comply. Supercharged cars of 1,500 cc and unsupercharged of 4,500 cc were allowed to race. The minimum race distance was reduced from 500 km (311 miles) to 300 km (186 miles). This set the stage for a world championship that was an answer to the World Motorcycle Championships that began in 1949.

In 1950, when the Silverstone Grand Prix was flagged off, a new era in motorsport had begun. It would be one of domination of certain names that would remain etched in our minds and frustrations of a few others who would leave no lesser marks. Alfa Romeo filled the first four places on that British GP grid and it would have finished with the chequered flag, but for Juan Manuel Fangio's retirement. He would go on to dominate this decade like no other, enjoying much success with Ferrari, Maserati, and Mercedes as well. But financial and safety concerns would mean that only Ferrari would survive going into the next decade, out of twenty constructors in the 1950s.

There were frustrations afoot as well. Stirling Moss came second behind Fangio on more than one occasion and would continue to do so, never winning a championship. Peter Collins would be another driver who sacrificed his chance at glory for Fangio, never winning a title himself. But the gravest concerns were those of safety. Various incidents where fans were hurt as well, most notably Le Mans in 1955,, who cast a shadow on motorsport. The machinery used was pre-Second World War to begin with. Alfa Romeo and Ferrari started with cars that were driven by Nuvolari and his like at some stage. They were front engine and used narrow tyre-treads. Things would change soon enough with the coming of Mercedes,

British GP (Silverstone), 1950; the first F1 race is flagged off

Previous pages: Mercedes leads Ascari (Ferrari); Italian GP, 1954 who would introduce full-body streamlined cars. Towards the end of the decade, with the rise of British interests in F1, cars would undergo a sea-change and take a step towards the future.

1950

Formula One, as we know it today, began with the British Grand Prix at Silverstone, with the royal family flagging off the race. Twenty one drivers and five manufacturers took part in the race which was won by Giuseppe 'Nino' Farina driving an Alfa Romeo. Alfa would go on to sweep the season, winning every race entered. Meanwhile, Ferrari ran their first F1 race in Monaco. In all seven races were contested as the championship next stopped at Indianapolis, Switzerland, Belgium, France, and Italy. Farina also became the first F1 champion, beating Juan Manuel Fangio by three points. Fangio was beset with technical problems all year and even led the final race, but for a seized gearbox to ruin his chances.

1950

At the season opening of Swiss GP, a British driver Stirling Moss made his debut. Meanwhile, Fangio won that race and overcame mechanical issues from the previous season, roaring to his first world title. But it wasn't as easy for Alfa Romeo as Ferrari were more challenging, especially in the hands of Alberto Ascari who won victory in Germany and Italy. But the Scuderia's first win came at Silverstone (where they missed racing in 1950) as Jose Froilan Gonzalez became the first Ferrari driver to win an F1 race. Despite them winning three out of the last four races, Fangio drove his Alfa Romeo to victory in the season-ending Spanish GP and took the crown. It was only fitting, for Alfa withdrew from racing owing to financial constraints.

Silverstone, England: The Italian driver Farina roars past the finish line to win the Grand Prix of Europe

1952

F1 got its first taste of politics as FIA reverted to Formula Two rules in the wake of Alfa Romeo pulling out. They did not want Ferrari to run away with the championship. Although there were many new entrants thanks to relaxed regulations, it is exactly what happened. Alberto Ascari won every race he entered with the exception of Indianapolis 500 where he helped Ferrari qualify for the first time, also a first instance for a European manufacturer. Meanwhile reigning champion Fangio drove for Maserati. But he broke his neck in a crash during a non-championship race in Monza, thus having to watch Ascari steamroll his way to a first world title.

British GP (Silverstone), 1953: Alberto Ascari first won for Ferrari here in 1952

Facing page: Juan Emmanuel Fangio skillfully maneuvers his Alfa Romeo car, May 20 1950, to take the Grand Prix of Monaco.

1953

Formula Two rules were persisted with and Ferrari were again dominant, winning everywhere, except in Italy where Fangio again tasted victory after 1951, a first for Maserati. Alberto Ascari drove his way to a second successive world championship, the first driver in history to do so, but he won 'only' five races for the Scuderia. The other two winners were Nino Farina (who moved to Ferrari after Alfa Romeo pulled out) in Germany, and Mike Hawthorn in France. Hawthorn became the first British driver to win an F1 race, having moved over from Cooper, for whom he debuted in 1952. The other 'first' of the season was a first F1 race outside of Europe. It was the season opener in Buenos Aires (Argentina) but the event was marred by spectator trouble when a nine-year-old boy trying to cross the track was hit by Farina. Nine people were killed in the ensuing mayhem. It was the first fatality in Formula One.

1954

This season saw the coming of Mercedes as constructor for the first time and they immediately signed up Fangio to drive for them. But the car was only going to be ready for the third race (in France) onwards. So Fangio drove the first two races in Argentina and Belgium, winning both of them, and this spurred his title challenge. The Mercedes W196 were full-bodied streamlined cars, and handled like a peach when Fangio took them to a first victory at Reims. But they couldn't cope with the quicker Silverstone track and for the rest of the season, Mercedes were forced to give up on the full-body cars, reverting to open-wheel bodies. This still didn't deter Fangio's challenge as he won six races and his second world title. Ascari wasted the year waiting for Lancia to bring out a worthy challenger to Mercedes. Meanwhile, Onofre Marimon was killed in practice for German GP at Nürburgring, becoming the first driver to be killed at a championship event.

1955

Stirling Moss had been rising steadily through the ranks and he moved to Mercedes to partner Fangio. It brought him his first win and that too at his home race, thus becoming the first British driver to win at Silverstone. In the same race, another British countryman, Jack Brabham made his F1 debut, driving for Cooper. Fangio had come in second at the British GP, but he won four races overall, thus becoming a three time world champion. However, the taste of victory was soured because great tragedies struck this season. Alberto Ascari was killed at Monza while testing a Ferrari sports car. About two weeks later, a mighty disaster occurred at Le Mans where Pierre Levegh's Mercedes crashed into the crowd, killing the driver and 80 other people. The French, German, Spanish, and Swiss GPs were all cancelled. In fact, racing would never return to Switzerland. Also, as a direct consequence, Mercedes withdrew from racing.

British GP (Silverstone), 1956: Fangio moved to Ferrari and won his fourth successive title

TRIVIA

Sir Stirling Moss is hailed as the best F1 driver never to have won a championship. He won 16 races in an eleven-year career, in an era where drivers did all the hard work. Despite this, drivers considered inferior to him have become World Champions. Moss finished second in the Drivers' standings in 1955, 1956, 1957, and 1958, and finished third in 1959, 1960, and 1961. He may have missed out on the title, but he was the first British driver to win his home Grand Prix.

Sir Stirling Moss (center)) wins the 1955 British GP

1956

After Mercedes pulled out, Fangio moved to Ferrari who were racing Lancia-make cars this season. Moss moved to Maserati and put up a strong challenge, finishing only three points behind him. But Fangio had generous help from his new team-mate, Peter Collins. Collins debuted in 1952 for HWM but won his first race at Spa (Belgium) that year, becoming the third British driver in three years to win an F1 race. The title fight went down to the wire at Monza (Italy) and Collins himself could have won the title had he won the race. But when Fangio was leading, he encountered steering trouble. Collins handed over his car to the three time champion, who went on to win his fourth world title. Collins though, would never win a title of his own.

1957

British racing was on an upswing and got a further boost when Moss joined Vanwall. He had always wanted to drive a car made in his country and their partnership reflected well in three race victories that season. But it wasn't enough to beat Fangio who had moved from Ferrari to Maserati and won his fifth (and final) world title;his fourth successive championship win. Moving away from Ferrari was the most prudent decision as the Scuderia was on a serious downward spiral. They did not win a race all season and two of their drivers, Eugenio Castellotti and Alfonso de Portago, were killed in non-championship events. But there was a ray of light at the end of the tunnel as Maserati folded up owing to lack of financial resources. Ferrari, despite their ill-luck, were still up and running.

DRIVERS CHAMPIONSHIPS

YEAR	RANK	DRIVER	TEAM	POINTS
1957	1	Juan Manuel Fangio	Maserati Maserati	46
	2	Stirling Moss	Vanwall	25
	3	Luigi Musso	Ferrari	16
	4	Mike Hawthorn	Ferrari	13
	5	Tony Brooks	Vanwall	11
1956	1	Juan Manuel Fangio	Ferrari	33
	2	Stirling Moss	Maserati	29
	3	Peter Collins	Ferrari	25
	4	Jean Behra	Maserati	22
	5	Pat Flaherty	Watson	8
1955	1	Juan Manuel Fangio	Mercedes	41
	2	Stirling Moss	Mercedes	23
	3	Eugenio Castelloti	Ferrari	12
	4	Maurice Trintignant	Ferrari	11.33
	5	Giuseppe Farina	Ferrari	10.33
1954	1	Juan Manuel Fangio	Mercedes	57.14
	2	Jose Froilan Gonzalez	Ferrari	57.14
	3	Mike Hawthorn	Ferrari	57.14
	4	Maurice Trintignant	Ferrari	57.14
	5	Karl Kling	Mercedes	57.14
1953	1	Alberto Ascari	Ferrari	47
	2	Giuseppe Farina	Maserati	32
	3	Juan Manuel Fangio	Ferrari	29
	4	Luigi Villoresi	Ferrari	17
	5	Jose Froilan Gonzalez	Ferrari	14.5
1952	1	Alberto Ascari	Ferrari	53.5
	2	Giuseppe Farina	Ferrari	27
	3	Piero Taruffi	Ferrari	22
	4	Rudi Fischer	Ferrari	10
	5	Mike Hawthorn	Cooper	10
1951	1	Juan Manuel Fangio	Alfa Romeo	37
	2	Jose Froilan Gonzalez	Ferrari	27
	3	Alberto Ascari	Ferrari	25
	4	Giuseppe Farina	Alfa Romeo	22
	5	Luigi Villoresi	Ferrari	18
1950	1	Giuseppe Farina	Alfa Romeo	30
	2	Luigi Fagioli	Alfa Romeo	28
	3	Juan Manuel Fangio	Alfa Romeo	27
	4	Louis Rosier	Talbot	13
	5	Alberto Ascari	Ferrari	11

LUCAS
AVO

1957-1967

THE BRITISH ERA

Although the basic formula remained unchanged, races were shortened from around 500 km/300miles to 300 km/200 miles and cars had to use Avgas instead of various fuel mixtures using methanol as the primary component. Then first the mid-engine and then the rear-engine cars brought about a change in thinking. As a result, power took a back seat and manoeuvrability became the watchword. Cars were deemed to go quicker as long as the driver handling them could push them easily.

Stirling Moss's victory in the 1958 Argentine GP was a turning point in that sense. Heavy and complex machinery found their days over in F1 and the cars became simpler, inviting the influx of many new teams into the sport. The most interested were the British and with quite a few world champions in this era, it was clearly their most dominant of the sport ever. It left an imprint which continues to this day, ever upholding the values of racing.

Engine specifications changed a few times in the second decade of F1 and it allowed for further growth. In an attempt to curb speeds, engines were downgraded to 1.5 litre, non-supercharged engines – a formula which would remain for the next five years. 1966 witnessed the return of more powerful engines, when the rules changed once again, allowing engines of 3.0 litre normally aspirated, or 1.5 litre supercharged capacity. The Ford-Cosworth DFV V8 engine would go on to dominate F1 for the next decade. Lotus were clear winners in the technology race and one of their greatest contributions would be the monocoque chassis introduced in 1962. Then, composite materials were first used in 1966, for example, an aluminium-wood laminate used by McLaren, and it single-handedly changed how engineers drove their cars, different from the space-frame designs of earlier days. It paved the way for more technological advancement and the coming years would only be a prelude to that.

Mike Hawthorn wins a dominant French GP in 1958 Previous pages: Fangio moved to Ferrari and won his fourth successive title, British GP (Silverstone), 1956

1958

Maserati and Juan Manuel Fangio's dual exit paved the way for British supremacy as Stirling Moss won the season opener in Argentina, driving a Cooper-Climax. It was a mid-engine car triumphing for the first time, ushering in a new era. Ironically he was on his way to the title at the final race at Casablanca (Morocco). But his team-mate, Tony Brooks, suffered a blown engine and Hawthorn eased into second position, winning the championship by one point. He was the first British F1 champion. Vanwall won the first ever constructors' title, but neither team would celebrate. Vanwall's Stuart Lewis-Evans died during the Moroccan GP, while Ferrari's Peter Collins had died during the German GP..

1959

The season began after a topsy-turvy winter. Mike Hawthorn died in a car accident in January and Vanwall pulled out, surprisingly. But the bigger news was Cooper-Climax coming up with a rear-engine car, as focus shifted to handling from power. Tony Brooks moved on to Ferrari and Stirling Moss would drive for both Cooper and BRM in British racing colours. It made for a terrific title fight, moving three-way between Jack Brabham, Moss, and Brooks, all winning two races each. Moss could have won that elusive title whilst leading in the season finale at Sebring (USA), but his gearbox failed. Bruce McLaren won his first race in which Cooper and Brooks finished third even as Brabham's car ran out of fuel. He pushed it over the line in fourth place and it was enough to secure both his and his team's first titles.

1960

Lotus came to the fore as Colin Chapman designed the first ever rear-engine car. The trio of Stirling Moss, Innes Ireland and Jim Clark, would take them to second in the constructors' championship. Chapman would also give a first drive to motorcycle champion John Surtees. Moss would go on to win in Monaco and USA, but he crashed during practice in the Belgian GP. Two other young British drivers – Chris Bristow and Alan Stacey – were killed during that event. Moss's accident allowed Jack Brabham and Bruce McLaren to run wild in their Cooper-Climax cars. Mclaren won the season opening Argentine GP while Brabham had a five-race victory run, including winning a fourth consecutive British GP, that handed him his second title. Ferrari lagged behind in the rear-engine formula and won only one race at Monza (Italy), that too because the British teams pulled out due to safety concerns.

Monaco GP (Monte Carlo), 1959: Jack Brabham rides to a first win for Cooper and later his first title victory

1961

The 1.5 litre engine was introduced and a lot changed as a result. Ferrari finally brought out their own rear-engine car as the British teams fell behind for once. Most affected were Lotus, unable to procure a new car, while Porsche made their first F1 appearance. They still finished second in the constructors' championship, thanks to Stirling Moss's two wins in Monaco and Germany, while teammate Innes Ireland won in USA. Ferrari drivers, though, made the season all their own. Wolfgang von Trips won the Dutch and British GPs, while eventual champion, Phil Hill also won twice in Belgium and Italy. But the most notable victory came for Giancarlo Baghetti, who at Reims (France), won on his F1 debut. Till date, he is the only one to have achieved this feat, discounting Nino Farina in 1950. However, the year ended tragically for the Scuderia as von Trips was killed at Monza (Italy), along with 12 other people, after a crash also involving Jim Clark's Lotus.

1962

Two things happened. Ferrari staff walked out on their team in the winter, leaving the Scuderia clutching at straws. They did not even enter the final two races. Meanwhile, Stirling Moss had an accident at Goodwood and suffered multiple injuries. He would never race again in F1. Jack Brabham formed his own team and left Bruce McLaren to lead Cooper. Lotus came out with a Monocoque Chassis for their new car, the 25, which was to further revolutionize F1 technology. Cooper-Lotus won four out of nine races while Porsche recorded their first win in France. But the season belonged to BRM for whom Graham Hill was in top form. He won in the Netherlands, Germany, Italy, and South Africa, the season finale. They won both titles after their first ever race win three season ago. But it would also remain their only success.

1963

Porsche withdrew to concentrate on sportscars and would only return twenty years later as engine suppliers. John Surtees moved to Ferrari and recorded a first victory at Nürburgring (Germany), a first win for the Scuderia, since 1961. The year saw phenomenal success for Jim Clark, who had won his first race a season ago, and Lotus as their pairing won seven out of ten races. With victories in Belgium, Netherlands, France, Britain, and Italy, he already clinched the title with three races to go. That didn't deter his form as he would win again in Mexico and South Africa. The other two exceptions would be victories for Graham Hill driving a BRM. It was simply the most dominant season for any one driver since Alberto Ascari won for Ferrari eleven years ago.

South African GP (East London), 1963: Jim Clark was in super form for Lotus, garnering five wins and the championship
The 1961 USA GP was the last Stirling Moss raced

1964

John Surtees created motorsport history as the first driver to win world titles in both two-wheel and four-wheel competitions. He had stayed on with Ferrari, who were in good shape with a new V8 engine. But it wasn't a dominant season for them, in the sense that three drivers went into the final race at Mexico with the championship in sight. Graham Hill with two wins in Monaco and USA for BRM, and Jim Clark with three wins in the Netherlands, Belgium and his home race in Britain for Lotus-Climax, were also in the fray. Surtees himself had won two races, in Germany and Italy, while his team-mate, Lorenzo Bandini, won in Austria. In fact, Surtees wouldn't have won the title without his help. Hill finished out of points and that left Clark to win the title, before he struck engine trouble with just two laps to go. Surtees was then let past by Bandini and he finished second to seal up his title victory.

1965

Lotus struck back at Ferrari with a new Climax V8 engine and the result was Jim Clark scoring a runaway title victory. He won six out of ten races, in South Africa, Belgium, France, Britain (for the fourth consecutive time), the Netherlands and Germany. Best six scores counted towards the championship that season and he had already sewn up the title with three races to run. Such was his dominance that he missed the second race in Monaco, going to compete in the Indianapolis 500, and won there as well, his victory being a first for a rear-engine car. The last three races saw three different winners. Graham Hill tasted victory in USA for BRM, but more prominent was his team-mate, Jackie Stewart's win in Italy. He finished third in the championship in his debut year. Ferrari finished winless as Honda, who debuted the previous year, won their first race in the season ending Mexican GP.

1966

A new 3-litre engine formula was introduced and everyone raced to get a car ready. Jack Brabham got there first, using a Repco V8 engine, and went on to become the first driver to win the title in a car bearing his own name. Having not won a race since 1960, he went on to win four races, in France, Britain, the Netherlands, and Germany. Bruce McLaren also started his own team but they only finished joint eighth in the constructors' championship. John Surtees started out the season with Ferrari, winning in Belgium, but fell out with the Scuderia mid-season and went on to race with Cooper-Climax. He would also win with them in the season finale in Mexico. Lotus struggled with the new engine regulations but would find a solution soon enough.

TRIVIA

One of the biggest technological moves came forth when Ford partnered with Team Lotus to develop fabled Cosworth F1 engine. A turning point came over in F1 history at the 1967 Dutch GP at Zandvoort marking the debut of the Ford Cosworth DFV 3.0 V8, the power plant that would go on to dominate the sport for nearly two decades.

Jim Clark, racing a Formula One car for Lotus-Climax, in a pit stop at the Italian Grand Prix in Monza

1967

Colin Chapman got Ford to invest in a new engine and they got Cosworth to come up with a V8 engine exclusively for the use of Lotus. It was the start of a new era, although championship results would take some time coming. He also got Graham Hill to join Jim Clark at his team which meant Jackie Stewart would be the lead driver at BRM. But none of this could deter Brabham as they rode their way to another championship. Only this time it was Denny Hulme who outshone his boss to take the drivers' title. Both of them would win two races each, but he had a more consistent year with six other podium finishes in comparison to Jack's four. In fact Hulme finished third behind him in Mexico sealing his championship. Jim Clark won that race as also three others in Netherlands, USA and Britain (for a fifth time in six years) but Lotus had far too many reliability issues to challenge for the title

Denny Hulme celebrates his win at the 1968 Italian GP
Facing pages: 1967 French GP (Le Mans): Start your engines!

toujours en tête avec
Esso
Esso
DUNLOP
DUNLOP

DRIVERS CHAMPIONSHIPS

YEAR	RANK	DRIVER	TEAM	POINTS
1967	1	Denny Hulme	Brabham	51
	2	Jack Brabham	Brabham	48
	3	Jim Clark	Lotus	41
	4	Chris Amon	Honda	20
	5	John Surtees	Ferrari	20
1966	1	Jack Brabham	Brabham	45
	2	John Surtees	Cooper	28
	3	Jochen Rindt	Cooper	24
	4	Denny Hulme	Brabham	18
	5	Graham Hill	BRM	17
1965	1	Jim Clark	Lotus	54
	2	Graham Hill	BRM	47
	3	Jackie Stewart	BRM	34
	4	Dan Gurney	Brabham	25
	5	John Surtees	Ferrari	17
1964	1	John Surtees	Ferrari	40
	2	Graham Hill	BRM	39
	3	Jim Clark	Lotus	32
	4	Richie Ginther	Ferrari	23
	5	Lorenzo Bandini	BRM	23
1963	1	Jim Clark	Lotus	63
	2	Richie Ginther	BRM	29
	3	Graham Hill	BRM	29
	4	John Surtees	Ferrari	22
	5	Dan Gurney	Brabham	19
1962	1	Graham Hill	BRM	52
	2	Bruce McLaren	Lotus	32
	3	Jim Clark	Cooper	30
	4	John Surtees	Lola	19
	5	Dan Gurney	Porsche	15
1961	1	Phil Hill	Ferrari	38
	2	Wolfgang von Trips	Ferrari	33
	3	Dan Gurney	Lotus	21
	4	Stirling Moss	Porsche	21
	5	Richie Ginther	Ferrari	16
1960	1	Jack Brabham	Cooper	43
	2	Bruce McLaren	Cooper	37
	3	Stirling Moss	Lotus	19
	4	Innes Ireland	Cooper	18
	5	Phil Hill	Cooper	16

CONSTRUCTORS CHAMPIONSHIPS

YEAR	RANK	TEAM	POINTS
1967	1	Brabham	102
	2	Lotus	56
	3	Cooper	37
1966	1	Brabham	65
	2	Cooper	49
	3	Ferrari	42
1965	1	BRM	81
	2	Lotus	66
	3	Brabham	44
1964	1	BRM	70
	2	Ferrari	64
	3	Lotus	52
1963	1	Lotus	78
	2	BRM	65
	3	Brabham	33
1962	1	BRM	62
	2	Cooper	45
	3	Lotus	43
1961	1	Ferrari	99
	2	Lotus	44
	3	Cooper	24
1960	1	Cooper	108
	2	Lotus	52
	3	Ferrari	43

DRIVERS CHAMPIONSHIPS

YEAR	RANK	DRIVER	TEAM	POINTS
1959	1	Jack Brabham	Cooper	34
	2	Tony Brooks	Ferrari	27
	3	Stirling Moss	Cooper	25.5
	4	Phil Hill	Ferrari	20
	5	Maurice Trintignant	Cooper	19
1958	1	Mike Hawthorn	Ferrari	49
	2	Stirling Moss	Vanwall	41
	3	Tony Brooks	Vanwall	24
	4	Roy Salvadori	Cooper	15
	5	Harry Schell	Ferrari	14

CONSTRUCTORS CHAMPIONSHIPS

YEAR	RANK	TEAM	POINTS
1959	1	Ferrari	97.5
	2	BRM	67
	3		22.5
1958	1	Ferrari	93
	2	Vanwall	60
	3	Cooper	38

GOOD YEAR
Beta
12
Agip
GOOD YEAR
Agip

THE WINGS AND GROUND EFFECT ERA

1968 - 1982

In hindsight, the first picture for present day Formula One was painted first in this era. Sponsorship arrived and left behind colourful liveries that would remain etched in our minds forever. The money that came in also allowed for driver movement between teams and therein the lure of technology for the engineers to develop something new.

It first gave birth to the aerofoils and wings, but the real step was taken with the coming of ground-effect cars. There were certain cars on the grid that were highly contentious, especially the fan-car from Brabham. That within three years of the first ground-effect cars coming on the scene, almost every team had them lined up on the grid, just pointed to the first of the races in technology. You just had to have what the other team had on their cars. It was to be the same with the turbocharged engines that followed, soon after. And it is easy to understand this urge, for in a highly competitive environment, lagging behind is not an option.

The one prominent effect of all this was F1 cars going faster and it led to questions about safety. Niki Lauda was the voice of concern amongst the drivers, especially regarding the Nürburgring track as it was becoming too dangerous to drive in its old, twisted manner. He knew it at its worst, having survived a burning car there and then later refused to race in precarious weather conditions, something unheard of until then. Races were cancelled for lack of safety for drivers and despite disappointment, it was an obvious formative step for the sport into the next decade.

British GP (Brands Hatch), 1972: Wings, a prominent feature in F1

Previous pages: Niki Lauda, driver for Ferrari in the 1975 Monaco Grand Prix at Monte-Carlo; he won the race

British GP (Brands Hatch), 1969: Despite safety concerns, wings on cars became the norm

1968

Early in the year, teams started experimenting with downforce-enhancing wings/aerofoils, which became standard soon enough. Sponsorship also first arrived in F1 when Lotus went from gold-green livery to red, white and gold of Gold Leaf cigarettes. Meanwhile, a new team would arrive on the scene, Ken Tyrell's Matra-Ford. They signed up Jackie Stewart as their lead driver and challenged Lotus for honours straight up. But the season would play out under tragic circumstances as Jim Clark, after winning the first race in South Africa, died in a Formula Two event at Hockenheim. His team-mate Graham Hill then went on to win his second championship, beating Stewart by 12 points, both winning three races. Stewart gave Matra-Ford their first win in the Netherlands after Bruce McLaren gave his team their first win in Belgium, two weeks earlier. Youngster Jackie Ickx would score his first victory at France, driving for Ferrari, their only one of the season.

TRIVIA

Bruce McLaren was one of the many drivers who lost their lives in this era

Motorsport has always been a life threatening exercise, and all who have raced for the pure thrill of racing need to be lauded for their bravery. F1 endured its worst years in terms of driver deaths in the Wings and Ground-Effects Era when new technological innovations every season made the cars quicker and mighty unstable. From 1968 to 1982, in fourteen seasons, 18 drivers including Lorenzo Bandini, Jochen Rindt, Francois Cevert, Jo Siffert, Ronnie Peterson, and Jacques Villenueve lost their lives on track.

Monaco GP, Monte Carlo, 1964; Graham Hill checks out his Lotus ahead of the race

Jochen Rindt died a World Champion

1969

Following wings, teams experimented with four-wheel drive, but it would not meet with same success. Wings too started having adverse effects on racing as they were high-mounted on the cars and could detach easily during events, leading to crashes. Lotus drivers Graham Hill and Jochem Rindt both crashed heavily during Spanish GP and the FIA promptly banned the wings for Monaco. The Belgian GP was cancelled. Later, in USA, Hill crashed heavily and although he was fit for the next season, he would never win a race again. The wings were back soon, attached to the cars' bodywork this time, and in future would shape the modern world of F1 racing. Meanwhile, Stewart won six of the first eight races taking his, and his team's, first world title in dominant fashion. Jacky Ickx (Brabham), Jochen Rindt (Lotus), and Denny Hulme (McLaren) won the last three races in Canada, USA, and Mexico respectively.

1970

An undesired first happened when Jochem Rindt became the first posthumous world champion. The season kicked off with Jack Brabham winning his first race since 1967, in South Africa. By March, Engineering were the new team on the block and Stewart won for them in only their second race, in Spain. From here on, Rindt took over and won five of the next six races. His new Lotus 72 dominated in Monaco, the Netherlands, France, Britain, and Germany. But two races later, in practice at Monza, Rindt crashed due to mechanical failure and died at age 28. Lotus withdrew from the event, but would win once more this season, with Emerson Fittipaldi taking a first victory in only his sixth race. Ickx won in Austria, Canada, and Mexico, three of the last five races, to set up a shot at the title. But Rindt had had accumulated enough points to stay atop. He wasn't the only fatality that year – Bruce McLaren had been killed earlier that year at Goodwood, while Piers Courage died at Zandvoort (the Netherlands).

1971

Jack Brabham retired and settled down as a full-time team owner, signing up Graham Hill to drive his team's Indy-derived gas turbine car. But Lotus wouldn't win a single race, a first time since 1960. Jackie Stewart moved on from March to Tyrell-Ford and Mario Andretti moved to Ferrari. But their original team would stay in place and one Ronnie Peterson drove for them, finishing second in the driver's championship although he didn't win a single race. Andretti won the season opener in South Africa and then Stewart took over the scene dominantly. He won at Barcelona and Monaco, then adding the French, British and German victories to his kitty. Ickx won in the Netherlands while BRM registered two wins in Italy and Austria, where Niki Lauda would make an unnoticed debut for March. Stewart won his sixth race of the season in Canada, replicating his form from 1969, on the way to a second driver's title.

Canadian GP (Mosport Park), 1971: Jackie Stewart continued his winning run with Tyrrell

1972

Lotus had a new sponsor, John Player Special, and replaced their green/gold livery for a black/gold one. Fittipaldi was now lead driver and they were up the table once again, back from the depths of the previous season. There were other new entrants on the scene; Marlboro sponsored BRM and Brabham was bought by Bernie Ecclestone. Their new driver, Carlos Reutemann, a first Argentine in F1 since the 1950s, took a stunning pole in the season opener at Buenos Aires. But Stewart won that race, though the championship would escape his grasp this year. Instead Fittipaldi would come to the fore in his Lotus 72. He won five races, in Spain, Belgium, Britain, Austria and Italy, the last one which won him the title. Meanwhile, BRM won their last ever race in Monaco, and it was ironical in the sense that their first race winner from 1959, Jo Bonnier, was killed in a crash at Le Mans.

1973

Graham Hill quit Brabham to set up his own team and Clay Regazzoni left Ferrari to join BRM, leaving Ickx to lead the Scuderia. He had a terrible accident in South Africa, where he was pulled out of the burning BRM in time. Lotus had two top drivers in Fittipaldi and Peterson but Stewart still won from them just like he had beaten pairing of Jochen Rindt and Hill in 1969. The title fight came down to Fittipaldi (Argentina, Brazil, and Spain) versus Stewart (South Africa, Belgium, and Monaco) as both won three races each by mid-season. Stewart stole a march as he won in Netherlands and Germany. In Austria then, Peterson let Fittipaldi through but he retired and Peterson still won. In the next race at Italy, Lotus were running one-two again, but Stewart charged through to finish fourth, taking the title. The season finale in USA was to be the champion's 100th and final race, but Francois Cevert was killed in practice and Tyrell withdrew from the event.

1974

Marlboro shifted allegiance to McLaren and were joined in by Texaco. This financed the move to lure Fittipaldi from Lotus. Ickx moved to take his place; meanwhile Niki Lauda and Regazzoni took up the seats at Ferrari. It was to be a keenly contested year as Reutemann took a first win for Brabham in four years in South Africa. He won twice more, in Austria and USA. Meanwhile, Fittipaldi and Regazzoni emerged as title rivals. The Scuderia driver won just the one race in Germany, but two wins for his team-mate Lauda and Lotus as well as Tyrell combining for five victories mixed up the championship real well. Fittipaldi fought back with a win in the penultimate round in Canada and it meant that both contenders had equal points going into the final round. But Regazzoni didnt finish in USA, leaving Fittipaldi to score a fourth place and his second driver's title. McLaren beat Ferrari in what was the first of many classic duels to come.

Monaco GP (Monte Carlo), 1974: Emerson Fittipaldi (McLaren) won his second world title that season

Monaco GP (Monte Carlo), 1975: Niki Lauda won the race and later the championship for Ferrari

1975

Lord Hesketh launched Team Hesketh for James Hunt the previous season and it bore fruit as the Briton won his first race at the Dutch GP. Meanwhile, Graham Hill quit his own team to move to Lola but he retired after the first two races. He was killed in November in a plane crash. Also, there were questions regarding safety at the Montjuich Park track where the Spanish GP was hosted. Several onlookers were killed when one of the wings from a car broke and flew across the barriers, bringing the race to an early end. Amidst all this, Lauda won Ferrari's first driver's title in eleven years, chalking up wins in Monaco, Belgium, Sweden, France, and USA. Fittipaldi won two races, in Argentina and Britain, the latter being his last victory ever.

1976

Fittipaldi quit McLaren who got Hunt for the drive after Hesketh withdrew. Tyrell announced a shocker: six-wheeled cars, and finished third in the Constructor's championship. Meanwhile the season turned out to be a most dramatic one. Ferrari won five of the first six races and Lauda accounted for four of those, in Brazil, South Africa, Belgium and Monaco. Team-mate Regazzoni won the first ever USA West GP, held on a street circuit, the first outside Monaco. Hunt won the Spanish GP and then was stripped of victory as his car was outside regulations. Lauda won his fifth race, taking the lead but crashed at Nürburgring (Germany) and was burnt severely. He made a remarkable recovery to race in Italy only a month later and finished fourth. Hunt won in Canada and USA, adding to his wins in the Netherlands and France, moving within three points of Lauda as the first ever Japanese GP beckoned. Lauda pulled out because of bad weather and Hunt finished third to take the title.

1977

Lotus brought out the 78, a first ground effect car with prominent sidepods, producing massive downforce. They won five races and would be a pointer towards the direction constructors would take soon. Renault brought out a V6 turbo-charged engine that would take F1 a step ahead. Talking of engines, Cosworth celebrated their 100th race victory when Jody Scheckter won for Wolf-Ford in Monaco. But it was followed by a spate of engine failures for their teams as the season progressed. Mario Andretti suffered the most, four times, and had only one win in the second half of the season. Lauda had only three wins and Ferrari weren't the quickest team out there, but given others' troubles, they were the most consistent. It helped him wrap up the title at Monza (Italy) after which he quit the Scuderia. Giles Villenueve came in and crashed in Japan, flipping his car over the barriers, killing two spectators.

USA GP West (Long Beach), 1977: Mario Andretti won the race in his path-breaking Lotus but the car was otherwise inconsistent

1978

Williams entered a customer chassis the previous season, but designed their first car as an independent F1 team. The Arrows team also came into being and the two finished joint ninth. Lotus introduced the 79 and Mario Andretti was joined by Ronnie Peterson who moved over after a disastrous season with Tyrell, who in turn discontinued the six-wheeled cars. By the Spanish GP, near halfway mark of the season, Lotus had scored four wins in seven races. Andretti won in Argentina, Belgium, and Spain, while Peterson won in South Africa. But other teams caught up, most of all Brabham who brought out their famous fan-car. Lauda won in Sweden and thereafter it was banned. It allowed Lotus to come back and no one could catch Andretti on his way to a first (and only) title. Villeneuve enjoyed a full season with Ferrari, though he finished 31 points behind team-mate Carlos Reutemann. But he won his first race in the season ending Canadian GP.

British GP (Brands Hatch), 1978: Mario Andretti drives away the radical ground effect car, Lotus 79

TRIVIA

The Brabham BT46B, otherwise known as the 'fan car', is the only F1 car to have a 100 percent winning record. It was the answer to Lotus's 78 and 79 models that made use of the ground effect concept. The BT46B used a fan to suck air from under then car's bodywork, providing a whole lot more downforce and it made the car go quicker than thought previously, Niki Lauda winning the 1978 Swedish GP and commenting that 'the wildest imaginable things could happen behind the wheel of a ground effect car'. Soon after, it was banned by the FIA, never to race again.

1979

Changes were afoot at Lotus, who now had Martini as lead sponsor. Reutemann moved over to partner Andretti, but the 80 wasn't the best car out there. Others had caught up, and indeed, built better cars as ground-effect became a rage. Jody Schekter quit Wolf to join Villeneuve at Ferrari and Keke Rosberg signed up to take his vacant seat. The Scuderia finished 38 points ahead of its nearest challenger in the Constructor's championship, but they were not overtly dominant, winning only six races. Schekter and Villeneuve split them four to two and took the title by four points. The first win for the Renault turbocharged engine was recorded at Dijon-Prenois (France) while Williams won their first ever race at Silverstone that year. In fact they would finish victors in five of the last seven races, a huge step-up in arguably only their second proper season.

1980

There was a reduction in the number of teams entering the fray as Wolf-Fittipaldi merged into one team. Alternately, Alfa Romeo came back to F1 with Marlboro sponsorship. Meanwhile Ferrari lost their way, much like Lotus did on winning the titles, so much so that Jody Schekter didn't even score a single win or podium. His best finish was a fifth place at USA West, where Nelson Piquet won for the first time. He had come in at Brabham to lead in place of Niki Lauda and won three races, the Dutch and Italian GPs being the other two. Meanwhile, Alan Jones and Williams carried over their form over and secured their first ever titles. Jones won in Argentina, France, Britain, and USA, as also the penultimate round in Canada. The championship was decided in Montreal when Piquet was penalized for a jump start and it cost him the race win. Jones, who had finished second, was handed the title on a platter. Outside the circuits, the teams were divided into two factions, Formula One Constructors' Association (FOCA) and Federation Internationale du Sport Automobiles (FISA). It came to a head at the Spanish GP where Ferrari, Renault, and Alfa didn't participate and the race didn't count towards the championship. Much of their politicking would affect races in the years to come.

Nelson Piquet won a close championship for Brabham in 1981

1981

Ferrari switched to V6 turbo-engines becoming the first team to follow in Renault's footsteps. McLaren were taken over by Ron Dennis and pioneered a carbon-fibre chassis. But they lost Alain Prost to Renault, who moved after only one season with them, owing to disagreements with management. Lotus came out with the twin-chassis 88 but it was considered to be outside the spirit of the rules and duly banned. Brabham too made a mockery of the rules, using contentious hydro-pneumatic suspension, but got away with it. The issue was bigger than any one team as side-skirts of F1 cars, which were an essential part of the whole ground-effect concept, were now close to being banned. The South African GP was again caught up in FOCA versus FISA wars and didn't count towards the championship. Meanwhile, there was much drama on-track as five drivers went into the last race at Las Vegas fighting for the title. Nelson Piquet led in his Brabham with three wins. Carlos Reutemann (two wins) was supposed to help Alan Jones (two wins) but launched his own title bid. Ligier-Matra's Jacques Laffite (one win) and Renault's Alain Prost (three wins) were the others in contention. Jones won the last race but Piquet came fifth, enough to secure his first title by one point.

1982

Niki Lauda was back in a McLaren while Keke Rosberg replaced Alan Jones at Williams. Ferrari and Renault protested over Brabham and Williams using a water tank to play with car weights, and Nelson Piquet's win in Brazil was cancelled with Alain Prost declared winner. Second-placed Rosberg was also disqualified. Because of that, politics intensified as FOCA teams boycotted the San Marino GP and only 14 cars entered the event. Tragedy struck in Belgium when Gilles Villeneuve clashed with Ferrari team-mate Didier Pironi and his car flipped, killing the Canadian. Pironi himself had an accident at Hockenheim later and it ended his career prematurely. Refuelling made a first ever appearance in F1 at Brands Hatch and it was introduced by Brabham, who made smaller fuel tanks and put on fresh tyres during the stop. With so much going on, there was much drama on-track as well, with eleven race winners in the season. Prost and Pironi were the only double race winners, but Rosberg with just the one win in Swiss GP (and five podium finishes) took the crown, becoming the first man since 1964 to do so.

TRIVIA

15 August 1982 was an important date in F1 history, when the Brabham team introduced re-fuelling during pitstops. It was the advent of racing strategy as we know it today. However pitstops already did exist in F1, primarily for working on the car or tyre changes. They had first appeared in 1908 at Targa Florio in Sicily. Pits were shallow emplacements dug by the side of the track where mechanics could labour with the detachable rims on early GP car tyres.

STATISTICS

DRIVERS CHAMPIONSHIPS

YEAR	RANK	DRIVER	TEAM	POINTS
1982	1	Keke Rosberg	Williams	44
	2	Didier Pironi	Ferrari	39
	3	John Watson	McLaren	39
	4	Alain Prost	Renault	34
	5	Niki Lauda	McLaren	30
1981	1	Nelson Piquet	Brabham	50
	2	Carlos Reutemann	Williams	49
	3	Alan Jones	Williams	46
	4	Jacques Laffite	Ligier	44
	5	Alain Prost	Renault	43
1980	1	Alan Jones	Williams	71
	2	Nelson Piquet	Brabham	54
	3	Carlos Reutemann	Williams	49
	4	Jacques Laffite	Ligier	34
	5	Didier Pironi	Ligier	32
1979	1	Jody Scheckter	Ferrari	60
	2	Gilles Villeneuve	Ferrari	53
	3	Alan Jones	Williams	43
	4	Jacques Laffite	Ligier	36
	5	Clay Regazzoni	Williams	32
1978	1	Mario Andretti	Lotus	64
	2	Ronnie Peterson	Lotus	51
	3	Carlos Reutemann	Ferrari	48
	4	Niki Lauda	Brabham	44
	5	Patrick Depailler	Tyrrell	34
1977	1	Niki Lauda	Ferrari	72
	2	Jody Scheckter	Wolf	55
	3	Mario Andretti	Lotus	47
	4	Carlos Reutemann	Ferrari	42
	5	James Hunt	McLaren	40
1976	1	James Hunt	McLaren	69
	2	Niki Lauda	Ferrari	68
	3	Jody Scheckter	Tyrrell	49
	4	Patrick Depailler	Tyrrell	39
	5	Clay Regazzoni	Ferrari	31
1975	1	Niki Lauda	Ferrari	64.5
	2	Emerson Fittipaldi	McLaren	45
	3	Carlos Reutemann	Brabham	37
	4	James Hunt	Hesketh	33
	5	Clay Regazzoni	Ferrari	25

CONSTRUCTORS CHAMPIONSHIPS

YEAR	RANK	TEAM	POINTS
1982	1	Ferrari	74
	2	McLaren	69
	3	Renault	62
1981	1	Williams	95
	2	Brabham	61
	3	Renault	54
1980	1	Williams	120
	2	Ligier	66
	3	Brabham	55
1979	1	Ferrari	113
	2	Williams	75
	3	Ligier	61
1978	1	Lotus	116
	2	Brabham	69
	3	Ferrari	65
1977	1	Ferrari	114
	2	Lotus	67
	3	McLaren	65
1976	1	Ferrari	99
	2	McLaren	88
	3	Tyrrell	88
1975	1	Ferrari	89.5
	2	McLaren	65
	3	Brabham	61

DRIVERS CHAMPIONSHIPS

YEAR	RANK	DRIVER	TEAM	POINTS
1974	1	Emerson Fittipaldi	McLaren	55
	2	Clay Regazzoni	Ferrari	52
	3	Jody Scheckter	Tyrrell	45
	4	Niki Lauda	Ferrari	38
	5	Ronnie Peterson	Lotus	35
1973	1	Jackie Stewart	Tyrrell	71
	2	Emerson Fittipaldi	Lotus	55
	3	Ronnie Peterson	Lotus	52
	4	Francois Cevert	Tyrrell	47
	5	Peter Revson	McLaren	38
1972	1	Emerson Fittipaldi	Lotus	61
	2	Jackie Stewart	Tyrrell	45
	3	Denny Hulme	McLaren	39
	4	Jacky Ickx	Ferrari	27
	5	Peter Revson	McLaren	23
1971	1	Jackie Stewart	Tyrrell	62
	2	Ronnie Peterson	March	33
	3	Francois Cevert	Tyrrell	26
	4	Jacky Ickx	Ferrari	19
	5	Jo Siffert	BRM	19
1970	1	Jochen Rindt	Lotus	45
	2	Jacky Ickx	Ferrari	40
	3	Clay Regazzoni	Ferrari	33
	4	Denny Hulme	McLaren	27
	5	Jackie Stewart	Tyrrell	25
1969	1	Jackie Stewart	Matra	63
	2	Jacky Ickx	Brabham	37
	3	Bruce McLaren	McLaren	26
	4	Jochen Rindt	Lotus	22
	5	Denny Hulme	Matra	20
1968	1	Graham Hill	Lotus	48
	2	Jackie Stewart	Matra	36
	3	Denny Hulme	McLaren	33
	4	Jacky Ickx	Ferrari	27
	5	Bruce McLaren	McLaren	22

CONSTRUCTORS CHAMPIONSHIPS

YEAR	RANK	TEAM	POINTS
1974	1	Ferrari	90
	2	McLaren	87
	3	Tyrrell	59
1973	1	Tyrrell	118
	2	Lotus	107
	3	McLaren	68
1972	1	McLaren	66
	2	Lotus	61
	3	Tyrrell	60
1971	1	Tyrrell	88
	2	Ferrari	44
	3	BRM	42
1970	1	Ferrari	76
	2	Lotus	70
	3	March	55
1969	1	Matra	86
	2	Brabham	65
	3	Lotus	57
1968	1	Lotus	75
	2	McLaren	64
	3	Matra	51

TURBO ERA

1983 - 1988

With title victory secured for Nelson Piquet's Brabham in 1983, the turbo era began in Formula One history. These engines had first been introduced by Renault towards the end of the last decade and quickly became the norm across the grid. After all, who didn't want extra power in their engines? It was power that could boost them up the grid, into the points, challenging for victories and the prize money that came with it.

Perhaps that was the bone of contention amongst the various competing teams who were now divided into two factions: FISA and FOCA. Time and again they had clashed over various issues, ranging from pay structure for the teams to bans pertaining to ground-effects. Led by Bernie Ecclestone, FOCA came out on top in this power struggle but it soon became clear to them that they would have to tow the line of FISA teams. By 1984, Tyrrell continued to struggle with non-turbo DFV engines but they too would fall in line soon enough. More could be seen from the fact that McLaren, a big playerin the FOCA line-up, got TAG engines especially to compete at the forefront of the championship.

Power achieved by the turbocharged cars could finally match the 640 hp (477 kW) produced by the supercharged 1937 Mercedes-Benz W125, without a huge consumption of very explosive special fuel. By 1986, some engines were producing over 1000 bhp (750 kW) in short bursts in qualifying. BMW's 1,000 bhp (750 kW) dynamometer was incapable of measuring the output of their qualifying engines, some estimates putting them close to 1,300 bhp (970 kW). The thirsty turbo engines briefly saw refuelling introduced into the sport, but this was banned for 1984. However a need for

German GP (Hockenheim), 1983: Turbo powered cars became the norm as ground effects gradually disappeared from sight
Previous pages: Renault turbo engines; a rage in the eighties

control was felt and therefore, first fuel consumption and then turbocharger boost were restricted to 4-bar in 1987 and later to 1.5-bar in 1988.

In 1986 every car on the grid had a turbo engine, but that was to be their final high point. Simply because it was being felt largely that turbo was not the way forward. A new engine formula had been introduced as per which these engines would be banned from the 1989 season and the couple of seasons leading up to that time would be intermediary years, also allowing for 3.5-litre atmospheric engines to be used in cars who wanted to follow this approach. For 1988, the last turbo year, only McLaren bothered to develop a new chassis. This was also the era where rising costs first became a problem. A direct consequence of this was felt on non-championship events which were last run in 1983. The Race of Champions at Brands Hatch was won by reigning world champion Keke Rosberg in a Williams-Cosworth, closely fending off American Danny Sullivan.

1983

FOCA versus FISA battle came to the fore, leading to the end of ground-effects in F1. Instead, turbo-engines became the norm and FIA banned aerodynamic skirts in a bid to slow down speeds. Flat-bottom cars and pit crews have been in fashion since then. Meanwhile Williams had to wait for a turbo-engine being developed by Honda, who returned to the sport with team Spirit. McLaren too waited for Porsche to provide them engines. Colin Chapman died but not before making one last grand move, securing Renault turbo-engines for Lotus. Brabham stuck with BMW and it bore fruit. Nelson Piquet won the opening race in Brazil but then the season became a duel between Alain Prost (Renault) and Rene Arnoux (Ferrari). Between them, they won seven races and when Prost won in Austria, with four races to go, he had a lead of 14 points. But Piquet won two of those, the Italian and European GPs, whilst finishing third in the last race in South Africa. It sealed his second title as Prost retired in three of the last four races.

1984

Teams were only allowed to use 220 litres of fuel per race, down from 250 litres, leading to cooling of fuel pre-race so that more could be squeezed into tanks. Prost stunned all as he returned to McLaren, Niki Lauda returned to partner him, armed with the new Porsche V6 turbo-engines they were the team to beat. When only two races were left to run, Lauda-Prost stood five-all in terms of wins, 54-52.5 in terms of points. Prost won both, the European GP at the new Nürburgring circuit and the Portuguese GP at Estoril. The turning point had come earlier at Monaco, where Lauda retired and Prost won. Meanwhile, Aryton Senna had debuted for team Toleman and took a first podium in his tenth race, finishing third in the British GP.

Niki Lauda (McLaren) wins the 1984 Portuguese GP and the third driver's title; team mate Alain Prost finished second.

1985

Tyrell got Renault engines, and by mid-season, the entire grid was lining up with turbo-engines. Mansell left Lotus to join Williams, and in-turn, they snapped up Aryton Senna. He set alight all qualifying sessions, taking pole seven times in sixteen races. He won twice, a first win in the Portuguese GP and then the Belgian GP. Arrows signed Gerhard Berger, while Rene Arnous fell out with Ferrari after first race and they got Stefan Johansson instead. His team-mate Michele Alboreto won two races and gave challenge to Alain Prost for the title, but he was unbeatable in the McLaren. He won in Brazil, Monaco, Britain, Austria, and Italy, that's five victories and four other podium-finishes in twelve races. Two races later, at Brands Hatch, he finished fourth to clinch his first world title. Team-mate Niki Lauda had a poor season, winning just the Dutch GP. It was his last race win as also the last event there.

1986

Fuel consumption was reduced to 195 litres per race from 220, though there were no caps on use during qualifying. Keke Rosberg replaced Lauda at McLaren, and Nelson Piquet moved to take his seat at Williams. He formed a potent partnership with Nigel Mansell, who scored two wins the last season. Williams went on to win the constructor's title, but the driver's championship saw high drama. Piquet began with a win in Brazil and then took three more victories, in Germany, Hungary, and Italy. But Mansell took over the title race with wins in Belgium, Canada, Britain, France, and Portugal. Prost won in San Marino, Monaco and then Austria. He was keeping pace only on the back of his seven podium-finishes as the fight went to Adelaide. Mansell was leading when his rear tyre blew and then Piquet pitted for a precautionary change, leaving Prost to pick up his fourth win, and unbelievably, his second title. Elsewhere, Senna scored another eight poles in sixteen races, as also two more wins.

1987

FIA took steps to reign in turbo-engines as development costs were spiralling. A new formula was announced for 1989 onwards: two interim years allowed for preparations. Teams not running turbo-engines immediately – Tyrrell, March, AGS and Larrousse – were contenders for Jim Clark (drivers) and Colin Chapman (constructors) cups. Tyrrell won both but hardly anyone noticed. Renault withdrew, and Lotus went with Honda while Benetton took on Ford engines. Gerhard Berger moved to Ferrari as Stefan Johansson moved to McLaren. Lotus and Williams introduced active suspension in their cars but the latter were more successful in getting the desired results, dominating constructor's championship again. Meanwhile, Mansell and Piquet fought out the driver's crown. Mansell took an early lead, winning three of the first seven races. Piquet started his fightback, winning in Germany, Hungary and Italy. Mansell won again, in Austria, and then back to back in Spain and Mexico, but Piquest's consistent podium-finishes had given him a 12-point lead going into Japan. Mansell crashed in qualifying and wouldn't race again in the season, crowning Piquet champion, who ironically didn't score in the last two races.

1988

This was to be the last turbo-engine year and only McLaren bothered to come up with a new chassis. With Honda engines they were unbeatable, winning 15 out of 16 races. Gerhard Berger won for Ferrari in Italy and that was the Scuderia's only third win in two seasons. Senna left Lotus to join Prost and it started a stunning rivalry, though McLaren gained, winning the constructor's title by 134 points. Prost won in Brazil as Senna was disqualified. There was more heartbreak as he retired in Monaco, and Prost won his second in three races. Senna fought back with wins in Canada and Detroit but Prost wouldn't finish below second all season, except when he didn't finish at all. At Monza, he had an engine failure and pulled out at Silverstone because of bad weather conditions. Senna meanwhile finished tenth in Italy, sixth in Portugal and fourth in Spain. But the turning point had come mid-season when he won four consecutive races in Britain, Germany, Hungary and Belgium. With eight wins over Prost's seven, Senna won his first title (only 11 best scores out of 16 counted), even though his team-mate had scored more points.

Detroit GP (Detroit), 1987: Ayrton Senna's last win for Lotus though it announced his ascension in F1

Facing page: Monaco GP (Monte Carlo), 1988: Ayrton Senna moved to McLaren to pair up with Alain Prost and F1's most volatile rivalry was born

TRIVIA

Apart from the Turbo engines, the biggest contribution of these F1 years was the Concorde Agreement. After the FISA-FOCA wars had come to the fore, threatening time and again to break up the sport, it was evident that a permanent solution needed to be found, not just amongst the teams but also to protect their interests as a whole. Thus was born the Concorde Agreement in 1981, a contract the FIA, the F1 teams (currently represented by the Formula One Teams Association (FOTA)) and Formula One Management Ltd., which dictates the terms by which the teams compete in races and take their share of the television revenues and prize money. There have been six separate Concorde Agreements since then, andall of whose terms are kept strictly secret.

Ayrton Senna negotiates his McLaren through the streets of Monte Carlo

DRIVERS CHAMPIONSHIPS

YEAR	RANK	DRIVER	TEAM	POINTS
1988	1	Alain Prost	McLaren	105
	2	Ayrton Senna	McLaren	94
	3	Gerhard Berger	Ferrari	41
	4	Thierry Boutsen	Benetton	27
	5	Michele Alboreto	Ferrari	24
1987	1	Nelson Piquet	Williams	76
	2	Nigel Mansell	Williams	61
	3	Ayrton Senna	Lotus	57
	4	Alain Prost	McLaren	46
	5	Gerhard Berger	Ferrari	36
1986	1	Alain Prost	McLaren	74
	2	Nigel Mansell	Williams	72
	3	Nelson Piquet	Williams	69
	4	Ayrton Senna	Lotus	55
	5	Stefan Johansson	Ferrari	23
1985	1	Alain Prost	McLaren	76
	2	Michele Alboreto	Ferrari	53
	3	Keke Rosberg	Williams	40
	4	Ayrton Senna	Lotus	38
	5	Elio de Angelis	Lotus	33
1984	1	Niki Lauda	McLaren	72
	2	Alain Prost	McLaren	71.5
	3	Elio de Angelis	Lotus	34
	4	Michele Alboreto	Ferrari	30.5
	5	Nelson Piquet	Brabham	29
1983	1	Nelson Piquet	Brabham	59
	2	Alain Prost	Renault	57
	3	Rene Arnoux	Ferrari	49
	4	Patrick Tambay	Ferrari	40
	5	Keke Rosberg	Williams	27

CONSTRUCTORS CHAMPIONSHIPS

YEAR	RANK	TEAM	POINTS
1988	1	McLaren	199
	2	Ferrari	65
	3	Benetton	39
1987	1	Williams	137
	2	McLaren	76
	3	Lotus	64
1986	1	Williams	141
	2	McLaren	96
	3	Lotus	58
1985	1	McLaren	90
	2	Ferrari	82
	3	Lotus	71
1984	1	McLaren	143.5
	2	Ferrari	57.5
	3	Lotus	47
1983	1	Ferrari	89
	2	Renault	79
	3	Brabham	76

Shell
COURTAULDS
Shell
BOSS

THE ACTIVE CARS ERA

1989-1993

The turbocharged engines were finally banned in 1989 and a new chapter began in Formula One history. It would be dominated by aerodynamic efficiency as engineers began to look for ways to design their cars in such a manner that they would go quicker still. A first step in this direction was the introduction of active cars, loaded with driver aids and thus strategy became a very important aspect of the race weekends. Refuelling at pit stops was reintroduced turning each race into a series of sprints. Active suspension was pioneered by Lotus in 1987, semi-automatic gearboxes were introduced by Ferrari in 1989, and Williams gave birth to the idea of traction control in 1991.

Some of these technologies were borrowed from contemporary road cars while others were developed for racing primarily and depending upon their utility did or did not find their way to the showroom. From a racing point of view, every new technological feature allowed the teams to go quicker, and attain higher speeds, but it came with a rider: teams had to start spending more money. It brought over another aspect to the sport – sponsorship. Lightweight cameras were attached to the cars following an American network TV practice. Along with boosting audience figures, this also made the sport more attractive to sponsors beyond the traditional cigarette companies.

Of course in the backdrop of all this, it seemed as if technology was once again driving the races and not the drivers and the FIA banned many such aids after receiving complaints in 1994. Even so, they did not have the technology or the methods to eliminate these features from competition, and no preventive actions were taken just yet.

Monaco GP (Monte Carlo), 1990: Ground effects and turbo engines gave way to active suspension as modern day F1 took shape
Previous pages: Senna checks his McLaren, Canadian GP, 1990

1989

New teams came in as 39 drivers competed for 26 slots on the grid, and an additional qualifying was held on practice Fridays. Nigel Mansell moved to Ferrari, leaving Williams, who took on Thierry Boutsen, whose seat at Benetton in-turn was taken by Johnny Herbert. Williams got Renault engines and Ferrari introduced semi-automatic gearboxes. Boutsen won in Canada and Australia, while Mansell won for Ferrari in Brazil and Hungary. Team-mate Gerhard Berger won in Portugal and Benetton's Alessandro Nannini won in Japan. Beyond that, McLaren won twelve of the sixteen races, taking successive constructors' titles. The Senna-Prost rivalry, however, grew bitter. Again, Senna won more races, six compared to Prost's four. But while he took seven other podiums, his Brazilian team-mate retired six times. After Senna won at Imola, passing him despite a pre-race agreement, Prost refused to talk to him. He then won at Monza and celebrated with Ferrari fans, clearly disenchanted with McLaren, leading Ron Dennis to express displeasure in public. The penultimate round at Suzuka (Japan) saw them clashing on track. Senna won, only to be disqualified later and Prost, who had retired, won his third drivers' title.

1990

Prost left McLaren to join Ferrari and Berger moved in the opposite direction. Piquet returned with Benetton on a performance based contract. Fuel suppliers introduced aromatics and trick fuels became fashionable in a bid to boost engine power. Senna had a run-in with FISA president Jean-Marie Balestre at the end of the previous season and for a brief period, it seemed as if he wouldn't be allowed entry into the championship. But once he was allowed in, Senna drove his way straight to the championship. He won six races, in USA, Monaco, Canada, Germany, Belgium, and Italy. It was one more than Prost who was giving him a tough chase, obviously. Scoring five wins for Ferrari in Brazil, Monaco, France, Britain, and Spain, he went into the penultimate round at Suzuka needing another favourable result. But it was was déjà vu, as the duo clashed again, both retiring this time, ending the title fight in Senna's favour.

Prost vs Senna: When matters came to a head between team-mates

1991

Nigel Mansell quit Ferrari to join Williams, while Jean Alesi moved to Ferrari to partner Prost. But the Scuderia experienced a poor season, not winning a single race. Benetton took on Mika Hakkinen while Eddie Jordan entered a team with his name on the chassis and Michael Schumacher in the car for the last six races. Meanwhile, McLaren had new Honda V12 engines, and Senna rode his way to four wins in the first four races, in USA, Brazil, San Marino, and Monaco. His luck ran out in Silverstone and Hockenheim literally, running out of fuel. Mansell won both those races as well as the first French GP at Magny-Cours, prior to push forth a title charge. Senna replied with wins in Belgium and Hungary to salvage his title hopes. In Portugal, two races later, came the turning point, when Mansell was disqualified for an illegal stop to re-apply his right rear wheel that had come loose during a pit-stop. Then he crashed out in Japan as Senna took second place, winning a second consecutive title and a third overall.

Nigel Mansell drives Senna back to the pits, also reflective of his dominating world title

1992

Ferrari replaced Alain Prost (away on sabbatical) with Italian Ivan Capelli to partner Jean Alesi. Jordan moved to Yamaha Power and finished 11th as compared to 5th in their debut season. Hakkinen moved to Lotus while Damon Hill debuted for Brabham. Williams' designers Patrick Head, and Adrian Newey gave Nigel Mansell a winning car, mated with a powerful Renault engine, including driver aids such as active suspension and traction control, allowing him to stamp his authority like never before. He won ten races out of sixteen and was on pole for eight of those, finishing a whopping 52 points ahead of second ranked Ricardo Patrese, his Williams team-mate. He wrapped up his first (and only) title with a second-place in Hungary, five races before the end, scoring 108 points in all. Senna won three races but finished only fourth, his limelight stolen by Michael Schumacher's first F1 win at Spa-Francorchamps (Belgium). The German finished third in the drivers' championship.

1993

Alain Prost came back to F1 with Williams, with Damon Hill as team-mate, paving the way for Mansell's exit. Senna sceptically stayed on at McLaren as Honda engines had been replaced by Ford. Michael Andretti replaced Gerhard Berger who left for Ferrari to partner Jean Alesi. Hakkinen spent a year away, waiting for Senna to quit McLaren, while Eddie Irvine and Rubens Barrichello found race seats with Jordan. With only 26 cars in contention, fastest 25 were allowed to race, but drivers were allowed to do only 12 laps each in both qualifying sessions. Fans expected another Prost-Senna battle and it appeared so as they both won three races each out of the first six. But from then Williams proved to be the better car. Prost won four consecutive races in Canada, France, Britain, and Germany, taking his season-haul to seven, clinching his fourth title with a second-place in Portugal and announcing his retirement. Thereafter, Senna won the last two races, five in all, including a sensational one in the rain at Donington Park, arguably hailed as the best F1 drive ever.

TRIVIA

A new era began in F1 history on 25 August 1991, when Michael Schumacher made his debut for Jordan Ford at the Belgian GP. In 2011, at Spa Francorchamps, when the German legend completed twenty years in F1, the man who gave him his first drive, Eddie Jordan, reminisced thus: 'I asked him, 'Have you been to Spa?', and he said, 'Yes'. And I should have asked, 'Have you raced at Spa?' If I'd found out that he hadn't raced, I don't think I'd have given him the drive.'

DRIVERS CHAMPIONSHIPS

YEAR	RANK	DRIVER	TEAM	POINTS
1993	1	Alain Prost	Williams	99
	2	Ayrton Senna	McLaren	73
	3	Damon Hill	Williams	69
	4	Michael Schumacher	Benetton	52
	5	Riccardo Patrese	Benetton	20
1992	1	Nigel Mansell	Williams	108
	2	Riccardo Patrese	Williams	56
	3	Michael Schumacher	Benetton	53
	4	Ayrton Senna	McLaren	50
	5	Gerhard Berger	McLaren	49
1991	1	Ayrton Senna	McLaren	96
	2	Nigel Mansell	Williams	72
	3	Riccardo Patrese	Williams	53
	4	Gerhard Berger	McLaren	43
	5	Alain Prost	Ferrari	34
1990	1	Ayrton Senna	McLaren	78
	2	Alain Prost	Ferrari	73
	3	Nelson Piquet	Benetton	44
	4	Gerhard Berger	McLaren	43
	5	Nigel Mansell	Ferrari	37
1989	1	Alain Prost	McLaren	81
	2	Ayrton Senna	McLaren	60
	3	Riccardo Patrese	Williams	40
	4	Nigel Mansell	Ferrari	38
	5	Thierry Boutsen	Williams	37

CONSTRUCTORS CHAMPIONSHIPS

YEAR	RANK	TEAM	POINTS
1993	1	Williams	168
	2	McLaren	84
	3	Benetton	72
1992	1	Williams	164
	2	McLaren	99
	3	Benetton	91
1991	1	McLaren	139
	2	Williams	125
	3	Ferrari	55.5
1990	1	McLaren	121
	2	Ferrari	110
	3	Benetton	71
1989	1	McLaren	141
	2	Williams	77
	3	Ferrari	59

Marlboro
vodafone
OLYMPUS
FIAT
Marlboro
vodafone
vodafone

THE SCHUMACHER ERA

1994-2006

The coming of Michael Schumacher to the forefront of Formula One coincided with several horrifying accidents and the death of Ayrton Senna and Roland Ratzenberger were the last straw. The FIA reacted swiftly with major changes to be enforced from that very season onwards, and it was the beginning of increased safety in F1. All cars' airboxes were required to be perforated to reduce their ram-air effect, to reduce power. Also, to reduce engine power, special racing fuels were banned, and only those with similar characteristics to everyday unleaded petrol were permitted. To reduce downforce, a wooden plank was to be fitted beneath the central portion of the chassis, forcing a large section of the floor further away from the track. If the plank was worn over a certain tolerance, the car was deemed illegal.

Further changes were mandated as the years went on, all in a bid to increase safety for all associated with the sport. Changes were made to curb the cars' speeds, increase in the size of cockpits, introduction of grooved tyres to reduce tyre grip, and wing elements were controlled andcomprehensive checks on car stiffness was introduced. All these rules came into being rapidly, one by one and sometimes that had an adverse effect in some of the teams. Michael Schumacher was perhaps the worst affected, as his Benetton car was found to be in breach of regulations on a number of occasions. He had to serve several penalties and fight race bans, and his 1994 championship will always be under the scan-

The driver-team pairing of Michael Schumacher and Ferrari dominated F1 like no other

Previous pages: Michael Schumacher chased by his brother, Ralf Schumacher during the Canadian GP

ner as a result.

The fag end of the nineties also signalled the end of the privateer era in Formula One. Renault withdrew from the sport for the umpteenth time. Brabham and Lotus vanished from the starting grid. Ligier was sold to Alain Prost and Tyrrell was sold to BAR. Jackier Stewart sold his team to Ford and then it was re-badged as Jaguar Racing. Other common names like Dallara, Simtek, Pacific and Forti vanished altogether while Jordan, Sauber, Arrows and Minardi managed to survive somehow. Later on, Prost and Arrows too had to shut down for good. However this did not deter Ferrari who were at the other end of the spectrum, reigning strong at the top of the podium. Even so, the ratings for the sport were at an all time low, signalling considerable trouble. Rule changes then began to be introduced every year for the fans' benefit. A new points system came into being first and when that did not stop Ferrari, qualifying rules were changed. Later, tyres were made to last whole race distances in 2005. That year also marked the end of the V10 era in Formula One. After the banning of turbocharged engines, in 1989, V10 became the most popular engine configuration in Formula One. To keep costs down, the configuration was made mandatory in 2000 so that engine builders would not develop and experiment with other configurations. It was a rule

Spanish GP (Barcelona), 1994: It all began that year, with Benetton

1994

Driver aids were banned, so active suspension, traction control, fully-automatic gear boxes and launch control went out. Re-fuelling was re-introduced for the first time after 1983. Senna signed for Williams, considered at that time by many as the reason why Prost retired. Mika Hakkinen teamed up with Martin Brundle at McLaren but their new Peugeot engines were very poor. The season was billed as a straight fight between Senna and Benetton's Michael Schumacher. Senna qualified on pole in the first two races and then retired, Schumacher won them both. In the third race at Imola (San Marino GP), Senna was killed after a high-speed crash. It wasn't the first fatality that weekend as Simtek's Roland Ratzenberger also crashed during qualifying and died. Schumacher won the re-started race, and also the next one in Monaco, in all winning eight races with two other second-place finishes. He even served a two-race ban for breaking grid order at Silverstone and therein Damon Hill tried to make a title charge. He won six races, cut the lead to just one point, and went into the final race at Adelaide, where Schumacher drove his already damaged car into Hill's car, retiring both of them and sealing his first drivers' title.

1995

Driver safety became of paramount importance and a host of rules to slow down the cars were introduced; front wings with endplates, reduction in size of diffusers, and wooden-planks affixed to under-sides of cars to reduce ground-effect. David Coulthard had taken up Senna's seat at Williams, and like them, Benetton moved to Renault for engines. So it was considered a straight fight between Schumacher and Hill. But the difference being that Williams handled like a charm and in comparison, Benetton cars were brutes. It testified Schumacher's driving prowess that he overcame Hill's challenge then to win his second drivers' title. In all, he won nine races, in Brazil, Spain, Monaco, France, Germany, Belgium, the European GP at Nürburgring, the first ever Pacific GP at TI circuit and also at Suzuka, both in Japan. The last three victories came in succession, sealing his second drivers' title, his 102 points standing tall over Hill's 69 and team-mate Johnny Herbert's 49.

San Marino GP (Imola), 1994: The most traumatic memory in F1, when Ayrton Senna crashed and died

1996

FIA mandated a much-larger minimum-size cockpit to further ensure driver safety. Ferrari played a master hand taking Michael Schumacher from Benetton. Eddie Irvine was his team-mate and Coulthard moved to McLaren to partner Hakkinen. Damon Hill too had a new team-mate in the IndyCar champion Jacques Villeneuve. With

Australian GP (Melbourne), 1996: While Michael Schumacher (right) found his feet at Ferrari, Damon Hill (left) and Jacques Villeneuve brought back-to-back titles for Williams (1996 & 1997)

Schumacher driving an ill-handling Ferrari and McLaren not yet on the pace with their Mercedes engines (acquired in 1995), Williams were all alone in the title fight. Hill saw it as an opportunity to follow in his world champion father's footsteps and stood victorious in eight races. He had to counter some ill-luck mid-season but would have been in danger only if Villeneuve put together a string of wins. He did win four races in the season to go with seven podium-finishes but Hill could not be denied. Meanwhile Schumacher won three races, a superlative drive in the wet in Spain, and another two in Belgium and Italy.

1997

Williams let Damon Hill go and replaced him with Heinz-Harald Frentzen. Hill found a drive with Arrows. Ralf Schumacher, Michael's younger brother, debuted for Jordan. Ferrari threw a kitchen sink at winning the championship as Michael's main battle was with Jacques Villeneuve and his Williams-Renault. McLaren sprung a surprise with Coulthard, taking victory in the season opener at Melbourne, their first since 1993. Then the battle began in earnest as Villeneuve won two of the next three races. Michael won at Monaco, fifth race, before winning in Canada and France with Villeneuve winning interim in Spain. The see-saw continued mid-year as Villeneuve won at Silverstone and Hungaroring, while Gerhard Berger (Benetton) won in Germany and Coulthard won again in Italy, throwing a spanner in the works. Michael won his fourth in Belgium before the turning point came at Nürburgring when Ralf crashed into his car, putting him out of the race. There was more drama as Villeneuve was disqualified from the penultimate race at Suzuka for not slowing under yellow flags. Williams did not protest, entering the final race at Jerez one point behind. There, Michael ploughed his car into Villeneuve and retired. The damaged Williams carried on and Villeneuve finished third to take the crown, as Hakkinen took his first win. Michael's second place finish was excluded from the championship listings.

1998

New rules were introduced with narrower chassis and grooved tyres becoming the norm. McLaren responded best and with a one-two finish in Australia, the championship seemed theirs already. It was controversial though, as Coulthard let Hakkinen pass for a win, proving beneficial for the Finn later on, as Michael Schumacher served up a challenge when Goodyear brought a wider tyre for Ferrari. Michael then had three successive victories in Canada, France, and Britain, the last of which he shouldn't have won because of a stop-go penalty. But he took it after crossing the chequered flag in the pits and an erroneous rule allowed him this exception. With wins in Hungary and Italy and a second-place behind Hakkinen at Nürburgring, Michael cut the lead to four points.

Marlboro
BRAKE
FIAT

TRIVIA

Michael and his younger brother, Ralf Schumacher, are the only brothers to win races in F1, and they were the first brothers to finish 1st and 2nd in the same race in the 2001 Canadian GP and there again (in switched order) in 2003. In a ten year career spanning from 1997 to 2007, Ralf raced for Jordan, Toyota and Williams-BMW winning six times in 182 races. The highest he finished in the Drivers' championship was fourth, in 2001 and 2002.

Japanese GP (Suzuka), 1998: Mika Hakkinen and McLaren rose to successive titles, snubbing both Ferrari and Williams

1999

Tyrell's time in F1 was over and they became British American Racing (BAR). Villeneuve moved over to drive for them and Ralf Schumacher took his place at Williams. Malaysian GP was first included in the calendar and it was a first step away from traditional circuits. Ferrari-McLaren were jousting again, only this time it was Eddie Irvine versus Hakkinen. Schumacher had started well, winning in San Marino and Monaco, but he crashed out at Silverstone and broke his leg, going out of contention. Mika Salo took his place at the Scuderia but Irvine led the charge against Hakkinen, who was on even keel with the German, having won thrice at the time of the latter's crash, in Brazil, Spain, and Canada. He then went on to win in Hungary as well. Irvine had won the season opener in Australia and then trailed Michael, but won in Austria, Germany and Malaysia thereafter. Schumacher had returned at Sepang, finishing second and preventing Hakkinen from closing the gap. But the Finn took victory at Suzuka, his fifth of the season guaranteeing his second title. At the end, privateer teams would cease to exist. Larrousse, Dallara, Simtek, Pacific, and Forti left owing to rising costs, but somehow Jordan, Sauber, Arrows, and Minardi managed to survive a little longer.

2000

Damon Hill retired while another British driver Jenson Button made his debut for Williams, who took on BMW engines, while BAR signed on Honda. Team Stewart became Jaguar Racing and Irvine drove for them. Rubens Barrichello moved in to partner Michael Schumacher at Ferrari. It was to be their year, pure and simple. Helping their cause were McLaren, suddenly a lot more fragile than previously. Hakkinen got pole in the first three races in Australia, Brazil and San Marino, but retired in the first two even as Michael won them all. He would win again at Montreal and Nürburgring, before seeing a mid-season slump with three consecutive retirements in France, Austria and Germany. Hakkinen took full advantage and closed the gap with two podiums and a win interim, and then went on to win in Hungary and Belgium. But Michael bounced back with second-place finishes there and then won the last four races, in Italy, USA, Japan and Malaysia, making it a no-contest. With victory in the penultimate round at Suzuka, Michael won his third drivers' title. But more importantly, it was Ferrari's first since Jody Schekter in 1979.

2001

McLaren, Williams, Benetton, Minardi, Prost, and Jaguar took on Michelin, challenging Bridgestone monopoly after Goodyear's exit in 1998. Renault supplied engines to Benetton and took over the team next season. Kimi Raikkonen debuted for Sauber as did Fernando Alonso for Minardi. As for the title battle there was little challenge for Michael Schumacher and Ferrari. McLaren were just not reliable enough for a championship bid, but what hurt them most was the ban on traction control being lifted. They could not master a system for their cars. So Michael took his second successive drivers' title (and fourth overall) with nine wins in seventeen races. He retired only twice, had five second-place podiums and the lowest he finished was fourth, in Italy. David Coulthard finished second overall, a massive 58 points adrift. Ralf Schumacher won three races for Williams, his first in San Marino, while debutant team-mate Juan Pablo Montoya also opened his account with a first win in Germany. Hakkinen won two races, but finished a disappointing fifth overall. He announced a year's sabbatical from F1, later turning to full retirement.

2002

Raikkonen moved to McLaren to take countryman Hakkinen's place and Felipe Massa stepped in at Sauber. Alonso moved to Renault as test driver who got Jarno Trulli from Jordan with Giancarlo Fisichella moving across. Mark Webber came to Minardi while Toyota came into F1 for a first time. Team Prost had been liquidated before the season started and mid-way through, Arrows collapsed as well. Apart from a 'small' debate over team-orders at Austria, Ferrari oversaw Michael Schumacher's dominant drive to a hat-trick of titles, and five overall. He finished on the podium in every single race, third in Malaysia being lowest. In all he won eleven races, breaking a record held jointly by himself (1995, 2000 and 2001) and Nigel Mansell (1992). With this stunning streak, he won the championship with six races to go, the shortest time possible. He also amassed 144 points, surpassing his own total from 2001, beating his team-mate and second-place overall Rubens Barrichello by a record 67 points.

Japanese GP (Suzuka), 2000: An emotional Michael Schumacher on winning his first championship with Ferrrari

Austrian GP (A1-Ring), 2002: Team orders only slightly dampened the Ferrari-Michael Schumacher onslaught

2003

Points were awarded to top eight finishers (10-8-6-5-4-3-2-1) instead of six. Also, one-shot qualifying was introduced, meaning drivers only had an out-lap, a hot-lap and an in-lap to set a time on Saturdays. It resulted in the closest title fight in years, a three-way between Ferrari, McLaren-Mercedes, and Williams-BMW. David Coulthard began with a win in Australia and team-mate Raikkonen scored his first win in Malaysia next. He stood second seven times and twice third, doing his title bid no harm. Montoya won two races, in Monaco and Germany, but was otherwise inconsistent compared to Kimi. Michael won four times, in San Marino, Spain, Austria and Canada, before finishing his lowest (eighth) in Hungary where Alonso became the youngest ever race winner. He then won in Italy and USA, dumping Montoya out of the title race at Indianapolis. Raikkonen needed to win at Suzuka but managed only second, as Barrichello won the season finale while Michael finished eighth, enough to secure his fourth drivers' title in a row (sixth overall) by two points. Ferrari won the constructors' title, with Williams second and McLaren third.

2004

Jaguar and Ford announced this to be their last season and withdrew from F1 in the end. McLaren and Williams saw a downturn in their fortunes, hence no one could pose a minimal challenge to Ferrari. Raikkonen won just once in Belgium as did Montoya in Brazil, with Renault's Jarno Trulli winning in Monaco. Ferrari accounted for the rest of the fifteen races in the season, winning the drivers' and constructors' titles for the fifth and sixth seasons in a row. Michael Schumacher dominated like never before, winning a record twelve of the first thirteen races, eventually finishing with thirteen victories and a record seventh drivers' crown. He finished with 148 points, 34 ahead of second-placed team-mate Rubens Barrichello as Ferrari won from BAR by a massive 143 points. The first ever Bahrain and Chinese GPs were also run this year.

2005

New rules were introduced; changing tyres during pit-stops was banned, and engines had to last two races. Ferrari's dominant run came to an end as Bridgestone couldn't cope, leaving Michelin teams to fight it out. Montoya moved to McLaren to partner Raikkonen while Renault were spearheaded by Alonso and Giancarlo Fisichella. The latter began dominating early, with Fisichella winning in Australia and then Alonso winning the next three races. Raikkonen bounced back with wins in Spain and Monaco, and could have made it three in a row but for a suspension-failure at Nürburgring. Alonso won but going into the second half of the season, McLaren were the quicker car. Raikkonen won in Canada, Hungary, Turkey (new race), Belgium and Japan, but reliability problems meant Alonso continued to march towards the title. The Spaniard seemed to be driving a bullet-proof Renault, retiring only once in Canada. He won six races in all, finished on the podium another eight times, with a third-place in the penultimate Japanese GP, making him the youngest ever F1 champion. Also, Renault became constructors' champions for the first time. Ferrari and Michael Schumacher just won the race in Indianapolis. India's Narain Karthikeyan, who made his F1 debut with Jordan-Toyota this season, finished fourth (out of six).

Belgian GP (Spa-Francorchamps), 2004: When Michael Schumacher became seven time F1 World Champion

1994
1995
2000
2001
2002
2003
2004
MICHAEL
7 VOLTE CAMPIONE
DEL MONDO PILOTI

2006

Minardi became Toro Rosso with Red Bull now operating two teams, BAR became Honda, Jordan became Midland first and Spyker later, and BMW took up Sauber. Super Aguri also came into being. FIA announced only one tyre supplier from 2007 and Michelin announced their withdrawal at the end of the season. Engines were downsized from 3000cc V10s to 2400cc V8s. There was also a battle for F1 ownership with Bernice Ecclestone managing to avoid the threat of a breakaway series, getting a new Concorde Agreement signed until 2012. Nico Rosberg made his debut for Williams, meanwhile Felipe Massa moved to Ferrari as Barrichello partnered Jenson Button at Honda. Button won his first race at Hungary, giving Honda their first win in F1 since 1967. Tyre changes during pit-stops were allowed again, allowing Ferrari to bounce back and challenge Renault. Alonso started well, winning two of the first three races. He won seven in all, four of them in a row mid-season to stay on course for a second successive title. Michael replied with victories at Imola and Nürburgring, but was penalized for blocking qualifying in Monaco. He countered Alonso's run with three successive victories in USA, France, and Germany, and later, scored an emotional victory at Monza (Italy) where he also announced his retirement at the end of the season. He won a seventh race in China, but retired next in Japan due to engine failure even as Alonso won. A second place finish behind Felipe Massa in Brazil gave Alonso his second world title. But Michael Schumacher capped his career (until then) with a stunning drive to fourth after a puncture had left him last.

Karthikeyan; The first Indian F1 driver

Facing page: Belgian GP (Spa-Francorchamps), 2004: When Michael Schumacher became a seventh time F1 World Champion

TRIVIA

Kimi Raikkonen (right) with Juan Pablo Montoya (left), and Michael Schumacher behind Bernie Ecclestone

Although Fernando Alonso is considered as the next complete driver after Michael Schumacher, it is widely believed that Kimi Raikkonen was the one who could have kept the German's tally well short of seven. That is if McLaren had provided him with a car that would finish races or even if their engines would not explode mid-race, both in 2001 and 2002. Kimi did run Michael very close in 2003, losing out on the title by just two points. He eventually did replace the outgoing German at Ferrari.

STATISTICS

DRIVERS CHAMPIONSHIPS

YEAR	RANK	DRIVER	TEAM	POINTS
2006	1	Fernando Alonso	Renault	134
	2	Michael Schumacher	Ferrari	121
	3	Felipe Massa	Ferrari	80
	4	Giancarlo Fisichella	Renault	72
	5	Kimi Raikkonen	McLaren	65
2005	1	Fernando Alonso	Renault	133
	2	Kimi Raikkonen	McLaren	112
	3	Michael Schumacher	Ferrari	62
	4	Juan Pablo Montoya	McLaren	60
	5	Giancarlo Fisichella	Renault	58
2004	1	Michael Schumacher	Ferrari	148
	2	Rubens Barrichello	Ferrari	114
	3	Jenson Button	BAR	85
	4	Fernando Alonso	Renault	59
	5	Juan Pablo Montoya	BMW	58
2003	1	Michael Schumacher	Ferrari	93
	2	Kimi Raikkonen	McLaren	91
	3	Juan Pablo Montoya	Williams	82
	4	Rubens Barrichello	Ferrari	65
	5	Ralf Schumacher	Williams	58
2002	1	Michael Schumacher	Ferrari	144
	2	Rubens Barrichello	Ferrari	77
	3	Juan Pablo Montoya	Williams	50
	4	Ralf Schumacher	Williams	42
	5	David Coulthard	McLaren	41
2001	1	Michael Schumacher	Ferrari	123
	2	David Coulthard	McLaren	65
	3	Rubens Barrichello	Ferrari	56
	4	Ralf Schumacher	Williams	49
	5	Mika Hakkinen	McLaren	37
2000	1	Michael Schumacher	Ferrari	108
	2	Mika Hakkinen	McLaren	89
	3	David Coulthard	McLaren	73
	4	Rubens Barrichello	Ferrari	62
	5	Ralf Schumacher	Williams	24
1999	1	Mika Hakkinen	McLaren	76
	2	Eddie Irvine	Ferrari	74
	3	Heinz-Harald Frentzen	Jordan	54
	4	David Coulthard	MCLaren	48
	5	Michael Schumacher	Ferrari	44

CONSTRUCTORS CHAMPIONSHIPS

YEAR	RANK	TEAM	POINTS
2006	1	Renault	206
	2	Ferrari	201
	3	McLaren	110
2005	1	Renault	191
	2	McLaren	182
	3	Ferrari	100
2004	1	Ferrari	262
	2	BAR	119
	3	Renault	105
2003	1	Ferrari	158
	2	Williams	144
	3	McLaren	142
2002	1	Ferrari	221
	2	Williams	92
	3	McLaren	65
2001	1	Ferrari	179
	2	McLaren	102
	3	Williams	80
2000	1	Ferrari	170
	2	McLaren	162
	3	Williams	36
1999	1	Ferrari	128
	2	McLaren	124
	3	Jordan	61

DRIVERS CHAMPIONSHIPS

YEAR	RANK	DRIVER	TEAM	POINTS
1998	1	Mika Hakkinen	McLaren	100
	2	Michael Schumacher	Ferrari	86
	3	David Coulthard	McLaren	56
	4	Eddie Irvine	Ferrari	47
	5	Jacques Villeneuve	Williams	21
1997	1	Jacques Villeneuve	Williams	81
	2	Heinz-Harald Frentzen	Williams	42
	3	Jean Alesi	McLaren	36
	4	David Coulthard	Benetton	36
	5	Gerhard Berger	Benetton	
1996	1	Damon Hill	Williams	97
	2	Jacques Villeneuve	Williams	78
	3	Michael Schumacher	Ferrari	59
	4	Jean Alesi	Benetton	47
	5	Mika Hakkinen	McLaren	31
1995	1	Michael Schumacher	Benetton	102
	2	Damon Hill	Williams	69
	3	David Coulthard	Williams	49
	4	Johnny Herbert	Benetton	45
	5	Jean Alesi	Ferrari	42
1994	1	Michael Schumacher	Benetton	92
	2	Damon Hill	Williams	91
	3	Gerhard Berger	Ferrari	41
	4	Mika Hakkinen	McLaren	26
	5	Jean Alesi	Ferrari	24

CONSTRUCTORS CHAMPIONSHIPS

YEAR	RANK	TEAM	POINTS
1998	1	McLaren	156
	2	Ferrari	133
	3	Williams	38
1997	1	Williams	123
	2	Ferrari	102
	3	Benetton	67
1996	1	Williams	175
	2	Ferrari	70
	3	Benetton	68
1995	1	Benetton	147
	2	Williams	118
	3	Ferrari	73
1994	1	Williams	118
	2	Benetton	103
	3	Ferrari	71

22
Virgin

COST CUTTING

2005 - 2010

The big worry for Formula One going ahead was the rising costs and not just in terms of spending for running the sport as a whole. Instead it was the growing disparity between the teams at the front and those lagging behind. The gap was increasing more and more, for the spending capabilities were different for different teams. F1 being a performance based sport, it only meant that a car could improve only if there was a good amount of budget to spend during the course of the season. Development would be a continuous process. The biggest indicator of things going wrong was the pulling out of some of the marquee names of the automobile sector during this period, namely Toyota, Honda, and BMW.

It began with the introduction of a single tyre supplier 2007 onwards and that was Bridgestone since Michelin ended their participation after 2006. Every team and driver was provided with a certain number of tyre sets per weekend. This was also extended to engines and gearboxes. While the number of engines used per season was restricted, engine freezing rules were put in place. The current formula is to extend till 2012 after which a new turbo-based engine formula is to be introduced in 2013. Energy recovery is also to feature in that new formula as part of the sport's initiative to go green. This is a major step up from the KERS systems that were first put in use in the 2009 season.

Since costs were high in using a common KERS system for all teams, its use was limited. The FIA though made compulsory the use of Electronic Control Unit. More homologation was kicked in from the 2009-2010 seasons when certain parts of the car such as the driver's survival cell,

Brazilian GP (Sao Paulo), 2007: Kimi Raikkonen's first Drivers' title
Previous pages: Jenson Button drove BrawnGP to a double championship in 2009

roll structures, all impact structures and the front and rear wheels, were all homologated and could not be worked upon by the teams during the course of the season. The use of spare cars was gradually phased out and only two cars could be used during any particular racing weekend. Also in-season testing was reduced to 30,000 km first in 2007 and 2008, and then totally banned from 2009 onwards.
A new Concorde Agreement came into place, running until 2012, and one of the major implications of this new pact was cost restriction. Refuelling during the race was abolished for the first season since 1993 while there was a limit set on the number of aerodynamic upgrades permitted over the course of a season and restrictions on the number of team personnel who attend a Grand Prix weekend. It allowed for the entry of new teams into the sport in the year 2010 and whether that was for the good of the sport remains to be seen.

2007

Michael Schumacher's exit meant Kimi Raikkonen moved to Ferrari and rookie Lewis Hamilton filled his seat at McLaren. Joining him from Renault was Fernando Alonso. Bridgestone became the sole tyre supplier, providing two compounds every weekend - hard and soft - both to be used during the race. Engine development was frozen under homologation terms and a confusing new safety car rule was employed. The championship was also blighted by an espionage saga wherein McLaren were found guilty of having possessed Ferrari technical details. Meanwhile, the racing was simply thrilling. The prodigal Lewis finished his first nine races on the podium, a record that included two wins in Canada and USA. He won again in Japan and Hungary, the latter being where his feud with Alonso broke out. The Spaniard was denied numero uno status in the team, leading to a bitter falling over the remainder season. He did win thrice, in Malaysia, Monaco, and Italy, keeping his title hopes alive. But the crown went to Raikkonen, bringing Ferrari their first and only title since Schumacher. Winning the season opener in Australia, France and Britain, he put in a late charge in Belgium, China and Brazil taking a one-point title victory over the feuding McLarens.

2008

Traction and launch control were banned; instead a standard Electronic Control Unit was introduced. Qualifying was divided into three parts of 20-minutes, 15-minutes, and 10-minutes, with drivers eliminated after each session. Minimum lap-times were to be adhered to in case of a safety car. Spyker team was bought over by Dr. Vijay Mallya and team Force India came into being. A bitter Fernando Alonso left McLaren, returning to Renault and Heikki Kovalainen moved in the opposite direction. In terms of racing thrills, the season went one better over the previous one, decided only in its last twenty seconds. Lewis Hamilton's wins in Australia, Monaco, Britain, Germany, and China with other podium finishes, meant he was leading the championship going into the final race at Brazil. But his rival was the homeboy Felipe Massa, who won in Bahrain, Turkey, France, Europe, and Belgium to keep abreast. In a thrilling finale at Interlagos, Massa won the race and Ferrari started celebrating only to realize that Hamilton overtook Toyota's Timo Glock on the second to last corner, in partially wet conditions. He became the youngest F1 champion while the Scuderia had to contend with the constructors' title.

Fernando Alonso moved to McLaren, but found rookie Lewis Hamilton too hot to handle

Button and Barrichello didn't expect to be celebrating at the beginning of 2009, but they did.

2009

Honda pulled out at the end of 2008 and with only four weeks to go for the new season, Ross Brawn bought it out, introducing the BrawnGP cars. They were quick out of the box, real quick, and all thanks to a certain loophole regarding diffusers that Brawn had been able to exploit. And so came the double diffuser BGP001 which enabled Jenson Button to win six races, in Australia, Malaysia, Bahrain, Spain, Monaco, and Turkey. Red Bull, under Adrian Newey, and spearheaded by Sebastian Vettel, had to settle for second but they put a valiant fight in the second half of the season, winning thrice in Britain, Japan, and Abu Dhabi. Meanwhile in-season testing had been banned to save costs as also slick tyres replaced grooved ones. Kinetic Energy Recovery Systems (KERS) were introduced and all teams couldn't use them due to costing reasons as also the imbalance they brought to cars. Felipe Massa was hurt in Hungary and missed most of the season, while Force India came to the fore when Giancarlo Fisichella scored their first pole in Belgium and then raced to second-place behind Kimi Raikkonen, who scored Ferrari's only win of the season.

2010

Ferrari replaced Kimi Raikkonen with Fernando Alonso and Jenson Button moved to McLaren, forming an all British alliance with Lewis Hamilton. BrawnGP became Mercedes GP, the marquee returning to F1 after a good six decades. Ross Brawn took over as team boss and he formed a potent driver partnership of Nico Rosberg and Michael Schumacher, who came out of retirement. KERS was banned for the season but F-ducts and double diffusers rose into prominence. Refuelling was banned for the first time since 1993. A new points system was introduced where top ten drivers earned points (25-18-15-12-10-8-6-4-2-1), instead of top eight previously. Also it was the longest season in history, with nineteen races in all. Meanwhile, Toyota and BMW withdrew from F1 and the latter became Sauber F1 once again. Thanks to cost restriction agreement, three new teams came into being: Lotus Racing, Virgin Racing, and HRT. No one driver was dominant in the early half of the season and mid-way through five of them were in contention. Then they began dropping out one by one, Jenson Button and Lewis Hamilton going out first. In the end, Alonso and the two Red Bull drivers were left to fight it out. Sebastian Vettel won three of the last four races, five in total, coming out on top in a see-saw battle until the last lap of the season

The new Number One in F1, 2010

DRIVERS CHAMPIONSHIPS

YEAR	RANK	DRIVER	TEAM	POINTS
2010	1	Sebastian Vettel	Red Bull	256
	2	Mark Weber	Red Bull	252
	3	Fernando Alonso	Ferrari	242
	4	Lewis Hamilton	McLaren	240
	5	Jenson Button	McLaren	214
2009	1	Jenson Button	BrawnGP	95
	2	Sebastian Vettel	Red Bull	84
	3	Rubens Barrichello	BrawnGP	77
	4	Mark Webber	Red Bull	69.5
	5	Lewis Hamilton	McLaren	49
2008	1	Lewis Hamilton	McLaren	98
	2	Felipe Massa	Ferrari	97
	3	Robert Kubica	BMW	75
	4	Kimi Raikkonen	Ferrari	75
	5	Fernando Alonso	Renault	61
2007	1	Kimi Raikkonen	Ferrari	110
	2	Fernando Alonso	McLaren	109
	3	Lewis Hamilton	McLaren	109
	4	Felipe Massa	Ferrari	94
	5	Nick Heidfeld	BMW	61

CONSTRUCTORS CHAMPIONSHIPS

YEAR	RANK	TEAM	POINTS
2010	1	Red Bull	498
	2	McLaren	454
	3	Ferrari	396
2009	1	Brawn	172
	2	Red Bull	153.5
	3	McLaren	71
2008	1	Ferrari	172
	2	McLaren	151
	3	BMW	135
2007	1	McLaren	218
	2	Ferrari	204
	3	BMW	101

MOËT
MOËT
MOËT
Marlboro
Shell

CHAMPIONS

Guissepe Farina

Grands Prix: 34
Wins: 5
Pole Positions: 5

Nationality: Italian
First Race: 1950 British Grand Prix
Last Race: 1955 Italian Grand Prix

World Titles: One (1950)
Teams driven for: Alfa Romeo, Ferrari

'He was like a high strung thoroughbred, capable of committing the most astonishing follies. As a consequence, he was a regular inmate of the hospital wards.' – Enzo Ferrari

As the first-ever race-winner and first world champion, Giuseppe Farina's place in history is unchallenged. But he was better known for his aggressive, almost reckless style of driving and his affinity for crashes. Ironically though his legacy would include a stylish driving technique – straight arms holding the steering wheel – copied by his many contemporaries and later passed onto future generations. Nino Farina was born in Turin, the hub of Italy's car manufacturing industry. He started driving competitively by age 19 but his first attempt ended in a crash; something that would eventually define him. Given his affluent background, he was able to rise well in the racing circles and drove for Alfa Romeo, Maserati, and Ferrari in his early years. It allowed him the company of Enzo Ferrari and Tazio Nuvolari, in whose company he learnt more and sharpened his skills. It shone through when he gave some top notch drives against the likes of Auto Union and Mercedes on his way to clinching the Italian championship consecutively in 1937, 1938 and 1939.

In 1950, Alfa Romeo asked him to lead their team, also including Juan Manuel Fangio and Liuigi Fagioli, in the inaugural F1 world championship. He won the first ever grand prix at Silverstone (Britain), and then won in Switzerland and Italy, in all winning three out of six races. Fangio won the other three races but was beset with reliability issues as Farina drove his way through to the title. A year later, while Fangio won his first title, he would only win the one race in Belgium and finished fourth overall. In 1952, when Alfa Romeo pulled out, Farina moved to Ferrari whose fortunes were on the rise. He wouldn't win a single race in a season dominated by Alberto Ascari, his team-mate, but would do so in Germany again the next year. In 1954, he suffered a horrendous crash at Monza where he was seriously burned. He recovered but needed morphine and painkillers to continue racing, later succumbing to pain and retiring in 1955. He was eventually killed in a road accident off Turin in 1966, when he was on his way to watching the French GP.

1950: Farina en-route to his first and only title

Previous pages: Ayrton Senna after winning the Belgian GP, 1991

FACT

Farina's wife, Elsa Giaretto, considered motor racing silly and dangerous, trying to persuade her husband to stop. Three days after their wedding, he flew to race in Argentina.

Alberto Ascari

Grands Prix: 32
Wins: 13
Pole Positions: 14

Nationality: Italian
First Race: 1950 Monaco Grand Prix
Last Race: 1955 Monaco Grand Prix

World Titles: Two (1952, 1953)
Teams driven for: Ferrari, Lancia

'Certainly Ascari was wonderfully good. He was, rather, better than good, he was very good indeed.' – Sir Stirling Moss

The tradition of winning at Ferrari started with Ascari

When he was born in 1918, his father Antonio Ascari was the reigning European champion. That he would go on to be a two-time F1 champion, and one of the most dominant ones at that, came as no wonder. His first car drive came about only in 1940 and it was a wonder that he had a precise style of driving despite this late advancement in his career. Nevertheless he took quick steps to recognition from here on and by 1949 was in contention for a prime drive when the F1 championship idea began to take shape.

He started out for Ferrari and stayed with them for nearly his entire career. In the first season he finished fifth in the championship but the Scuderia were only getting started. In 1951, he recorded his first race win at Germany and then won in Italy, giving strong competition to Juan Manuel Fangio for the title. He eventually finished second but went one better the next season. Winning six out of seven races, he became champion in 1952 and then replicated the feat with five race wins in 1953, the first double champion in F1 history. He became a popular champion and was endeared to one and all down the pitlane. Equally well known was his penchant for superstitions. In 1954, he moved on to Lancia stating publicly that the move was for want of money. But they were not ready with their car till late in the year and his season never took off. Ferrari and Lancia were mated in 1955 and he continued driving for the unified team. But he had a near fatal accident at Monaco GP where he crashed at the harbour and his car sank in the Mediterranean. He survived but four days later was killed at Monza in a freak accident whilst testing a sports car. He wasn't wearing his blue helmet that day, instead racing with a borrowed white one.

FACT

Like his father, Alberto Ascari died on the 26th of a month, at the age of 36, four days after they had walked away from an accident. It was an eerily uncanny coincidence.

Juan Manuel Fangio

Grands Prix: 51 Wins: 23 Pole Positions: 27	Nationality: Argentine First Race: 1950 British Grand Prix Last Race: 1958 French Grand Prix	World Titles: Five (1951, 1954, 1955, 1956, 1957) Teams driven for: Alfa Romeo, Maserati, Mercedes, Ferrari

'Even if I or someone else can equal or beat Fangio's record, it still will not compare with his achievement.'
– Ayrton Senna

Fangio: The first truly dominant World Champion in F1

Known as 'Old Man' and 'Maestro', Juan Manuel Fangio was the first ever five-time Formula One world champion. And he achieved this feat driving for four different teams in the first seven years of the championship. It is to say that he was one of the greatest ever to have graced motorsport, perhaps eclipsed only by the supreme talent of Ayrton Senna and the dominance of Michael Schumacher.

He was of humble origins, born to Italian parents who migrated early to Argentina. There he grew up to be a mechanic and got a first race experience riding with a customer who frequented his garage. Gradually, he moved to racing himself and learnt his wares at long distance racing, overcoming hazardous distances in heavy cars, rally-style. It was a highly successful stint for him, and put him on course for further glory, when he decided to check out the European racing scene.

He got there at a relative late age of 38 years, and that too by the grace of the Argentine government and support from the Argentine Automobile Club. Impressed by his refined style of driving and the ability to handle heavy racing car of those days without crashing much, Alfa Romeo gave him a drive for the inaugural season. He missed out in 1950, but came back to win his first title the following season. He suffered a horrible crash early in 1952 - the only serious one of his career - that put him out of contention that season and much of 1953 as well.

When Mercedes entered the sport a year later, they signed him and he duly won his second title, although that also came because he had driver for Maserati that same season. A third title followed in 1955, also with Mercedes, but after their withdrawal at the end of that season, he moved to Ferrari in 1956. It yielded his fourth drivers' crown and then a fifth in 1957, this time with Maserati. It was clinched at Nürburgring, considered to be his greatest race, where he drove like a maniac after a late fuel stop to clinch victory. He did start the 1958 season but retired after four races. But his record stood for another 46 years. He died in 1995, at home in Argentina, aged 84.

FACT

In 1958, Juan Manuel Fangio was kidnapped in Cuba by members of Fidel Castro's revolutionary movement to draw attention to their cause. He was later released unharmed.

Jack Brabham

Grands Prix: 51 Wins: 23 Pole Positions: 27	Nationality: Australian First Race: 1955 British Grand Prix Last Race: 1970 Mexican Grand Prix	World Titles: Five (1951, 1954, 1955, 1956, 1957) Teams driven for: Alfa Romeo, Maserati, Mercedes, Ferrari

'I really should have won the championship in 1970.'

The first ever Formula One driver to be knighted, Jack Brabham was everything this sport could ask for. He was a racing driver, yes, but adding to that skill, his engineering expertise, team leadership and later nurturing new talent made him an all-round presence in motorsport history. Later he was the first to get into the business side of things, looking into sponsorship for his racing entries as early as 1954.

He was born in 1926 to a humble family. His father was a grocery man. But he studied engineering and then worked at a garage, later joining the Royal Australian Air Force. There he worked as a flight mechanic. In1946, he opened his own engineering firm. Two years later, he started racing professionally and that too in his own built cars. He was fascinated by the European racing scene and after winning the Australian Hill-Climb championship in a Cooper, met with the cars' constructors, John and Charles Cooper. It led to a partnership that would change the course of F1 history. Cooper became the first team to take the rear-engine path and the resultant was the onset of a new era. Until then, heavy, racing cars with front engines had dominated the scene but it was all about to change. Jack first raced a full F1 season in 1958, for Cooper, and a fourth-place finish in Monaco was his best result. The team though got a win through Stirling Moss, whom he would beat to win the championship next season. With victories in Monaco and Britain, and a consistent run of results – three other podiums – saw him clinch his first drivers' title. It also meant a first constructors' championship for Cooper and it only got better the next year. In 1960, the Brabham-Cooper combine was thoroughly dominant and won five races out of nine, grabbing a second consecutive championship. 1961 saw the advent of a new engine formula and Ferrari took over. So that was the end of the road Brabham and Cooper as he took the opportunity to set up Motor Racing Developments with his designer friend, Ron Tauranac. For the 1962 season they started working on a Brabham chassis and until that was ready, Jack raced in a Lotus entry. The first Brabham F1 car debuted in Germany, and a fourth-place finish at Watkins Glen was the first time a driver garnered points driving a car in his own name. However it wasn't until 1964 that they won a first race. But it wasn't Brabham to do the honours as Dan Gurney won in France and Mexico. Things changed in 1966, though when the new 3-litre engine regulations came in. Brabham got Repco to make F1 engines and fine tuned them into the chassis himself. He won in Netherlands, France, Britain, and Germany, going on to win his third championship. And a first for an F1 driver in a team bearing his own name!

His final victory came in the 1970 South African GP and at 44, he retired that season. Later the Brabham team was sold to Bernie Ecclestone. In 1985, he was knighted for his immense contribution to motorsport.

FACT

Jack Brabham's first drivers' title came in dramatic style. At Sebring (USA) his car ran out of fuel and he pushed it over the finish line, fourth, sealing the championship.

Mike Hawthorn

Grands Prix: 45 Wins: 3 Pole Positions: 4	Nationality: British First Race: 1952 Belgian Grand Prix Last Race: 1958 Moroccan Grand Prix	World Titles: One (1958) Teams driven for: LD Hawthorn, AHM Bryde, Ferrari, Vanwall, BRM

'For much of his young life Mike Hawthorn was shitfaced, about to get shitfaced, or recovering from being shitfaced.' – Charles Jennings in *Burning Rubber*

Hawthorn: F1's eternal playboy–1957

Mike Hawthorn was the first ever British Formula One Champion, and the title suited his personality – flamboyant, big, bullish and fun-loving. If Stirling Moss was the name that failed to complete the promise of his talent, by plan or coincidence, then Hawthorn simply kept his date with destiny. He was born to a motorsport loving family, his father purchasing a garage near Brooklands shortly after his birth. The atmosphere around young Mike then was always of competition with other cars and bikes, fuelled by his father who egged him on for pursuing his love of racing. In 1950 he entered the Brighton speed trials and won his first races in a small sportscar his father built for him. The year 1952 changed his life, when racing on Easter at Goodwood, he drove to victory in a Formula Two cap and beat the likes of Juan Manuel Fangio, He scored in every race on the calendar and finished fourth overall, but the highpoint of the season was his first victory in the French GP. Fangio was again the man beaten at Reims with the Scuderia just inches ahead. 1954 though turned out to be a bad year – first, he was injured gravely in a non-championship race in Italy, and then, his father died. He would carry on, salvaging the year with a win in the finale at Pedrables (Spain). But it was the start of a serious downturn as he left Ferrari at the end of the season. In 1955 he raced for Vanwall and then for BRM in 1956. But success would only come his way, away from the F1 scene at the 1955 Le Mans 24 hour sportscar race. Even so, his victory would be tainted for a Mercedes car crashed into the crowd at that event, killing 80 spectators. Hawthorn was one of the drivers blamed squarely for the mess, as he clashed with Pierre Levegh's car that triggered the incident.

In 1957, Mike returned to Ferrari to swing around his fortunes once again. He finished third at Silverstone and then second in the German GP. Next year would be the one for him, as with victory at Reims (France) and five other second-placed finishes, he won the drivers' title. Stirling Moss with four wins and Tony Brooks with three were also in the hunt, but gave way to Mike's consistency. However that season too was blighted for his team-mate Peter Collins died at Nürburgring, leaving the champion disillusioned with motorsport. He retired at the end of the season but in January 1959, was killed in a car-crash near his home. He was only 29

FACT

Mike Hawthorn always raced in his everyday clothes, usually a sports jacket and a tie. For F1 however, he bought white overalls and wore the bow tie that became his trademark.

Phil Hill

Grands Prix: 49	Nationality: American	World Titles: One (1961)
Wins: 3	First Race: 1958 French Grand Prix	Teams driven for: Maserati, Ferrari, Cooper, Porsche,
Pole Positions: 6	Last Race: 1966 Italian Grand Prix	Automobili Turismo e Sport, Lotus, Eagle

'Racing makes me selfish, irritable, defensive. If I could get out of this sport with any ego left I would.'

Phill Hill (Ferrari) making a pitstop during 1962 German GP

Perhaps the least well known of all Formula One champions, Phil Hill was the first American to become world champion. His title, many argue, was down to an excellent season for Ferrari who were quick to adapt to the new regulations that came into existence that year. However his title was over shadowed by the death of his team-mate Wolfgang Von Trips, much like his racing career, which was pre-occupied by the balance of racing and crashes.

He was born in Miami to a prominent family in 1927, and though he wasn't overtly good at sports, he soon developed a fascination for cars. He was gifted a Model T Ford by an aunt and he took apart that toy many a times to understand properly how it functioned. His aunt's chauffer also taught him how to drive, as he began taking baby steps towards a racing career. A definite change in his life came when he gave up studying at the University of California and started working as a mechanic in a Los Angeles garage. He raced first in 1947, in a car he modified himself. Later, tragedy struck in 1951, when he lost both his parents. But they had left him enough money to buy a Ferrari, and go racing with more ambition.

In 1955, he raced for Ferrari at Le Mans and was witness to the horrific incident there, one which would deeply trouble his mind for years to come. Enzo Ferrari finally gave him that chance in 1958 after both Luigi Musso and Peter Collins were killed. He helped Mike Hawthorn win the title that year and in 1959, his first full season, finished on the podium a couple of times. Later in 1960 he came to the fore at Monza, winning his first F1 race, but that was also an event marred by controversy as all the rear-engined British cars boycotted the event due to safety concerns.

With the new 1.5 litre engine formula coming in 1961, Ferrari were unbeatable and the championship eventually became a two-way battle between Hill and his team-mate von Trips. But again the latter was a sad event as von Trips crashed into the crowd, an incident that killed him and 14 spectators. Hill won the championship by a single point over his dead team-mate. Thereafter, his career went downhill, first with a poor season in 1962 and then leaving Ferrari during the winter due to a management walk-out. He moved to A.T.S and then to Cooper ,but could not challenge for wins, before retiring from F1 in 1964. He died in 2008, aged 81.

FACT

Phil Hill cast a very nervous persona pre-race. On the starting grid, he paced to and fro, endlessly polishing his goggles, chain-smoking cigarettes or feverishly chewing gum.

Graham Hill

Grands Prix: 179
Wins: 14
Pole Positions: 13

Nationality: British
First Race: 1958 Monaco Grand Prix
Last Race: 1975 Monaco Grand Prix

World Titles: Two (1962, 1968)
Teams driven for: Brabham, BRM, Lola, Hill, Lotus, Shadow

'I am an artist. The track is my canvas, and the car is my brush.'

One of the most revered Formula One world champions was Graham Hill. Naturally media-savvy, he enjoyed being in the limelight and had a huge fan following wherever he went. Known as a determined and intense racer, he made a perfect figurine for the sport. He is the only man to have won the F1 world championship, the Indy 500 and the Le Mans 24 Hours.

He was born in London in 1929 and grew up in the backdrop of first the recession and then the Second World War. He enjoyed technical education at school and apprenticed for the Smith instrument company. It was only in 1952 that he got a first taste for racing at the London Rowing Club, and would later wear the club's insignia on his racing helmet. Motorsport then came to him when he drove an F3 car around Brands Hatch. He then quit his job at Smith's and went to work as a mechanic at a racing school, taking part in races on pay-basis by the mid-fifties.

Then in 1958, Graham Hill became a Formula One driver with Team Lotus. But their cars were unreliable that year as also the next. This meant Hill now moved on to BRM and although it seemed like a bad move given their patchy racing history, it started coming together in 1960. He finished second at Zandvoort which showed there was some merit in his motives, but 1961 didn't bring about the expected results. Then in 1962, he won in Holland, Germany, Italy and then beat Jim Clark's Lotus at the finale in South Africa, thus winning his first world title.

The true World Champion

From here on, the slide started again for BRM and although he won the Indy 500 and three other F1 podiums with them in 1966, Hill decided to re-join Lotus in 1967. It resulted in a potent partnership with Jim Clark who was the leading F1 driver at that time. But a season later he was killed and Hill was now the leader at Team Lotus. He won in Spain, Monaco and Mexico that year, securing his second drivers' title. In 1969, he won the Monaco GP for a record fifth time, but was overshadowed by his new team-mate Jochen Rindt. Later, Hill suffered a crash at Watkins Glen, breaking both his legs and it began a downward spiral for his racing career. He returned from injury, but would never win again, undergoing some poor seasons with Lotus (1970) and then Brabham (1971 & 1972). He died in a plane crash in November that year.

FACT

Graham Hill was never a natural diver and only passed his driving test at age 24. He didn't have a valid driving license when he first drove at Brands Hatch in 1953.

Jim Clark

Grands Prix: 72
Wins: 25
Pole Positions: 33

Nationality: British
First Race: 1960 Dutch Grand Prix
Last Race: 1968 South African Grand Prix

World Titles: Two (1963, 1965)
Teams driven for: Lotus

'He was so smooth, he was so clean, he drove with such finesse; he never bullied a racing car, he sort of caressed it into doing the things he wanted it to do.' – Sir Jackie Stewart

To go from a farm boy to world champion in Formula One was quite a meteoric rise for Jim Clark. Born on 4 March 1936, he grew up with four sisters at a farm in Scotland's Berwickshire hills. At age 13, when he went to school, he was still quite far away from the world of racing as cricket and hockey took most of his time. His first drives included the family car and then the tractor around the vast empty space that surrounded him, after he had quit school to work on the farm. Racing came to him when one of his sisters got married to a local rally racer and it brought opportunities for him to witness rallies and indeed compete in a few races. He graduated to winning club-level events soon enough and then rose further with the aid of friends and well wishers. One of his friends Ian Scott Watson lent him a DKW and then a Porsche to compete.

Clark then tried his level best to go professional but a chance to race in F1 with Aston Martin didn't materialise. However in 1958, he drove a Lotus-make car at Brands Hatch and impressed Colin Chapman enough who invited him to drive in the Lotus Formula Junior. By 1960, he was driving in the second half of the F1 season for Team Lotus, though his debut season was marred by the deaths of Chris Bristow and team-mate Alan Stacey, both drying at Spa. His first full season, in 1961, too witnessed tragedy. At Monza, he collided with Wolfgang Von Trips' Ferrari and

Jim Clark (Lotus) in action at the 1964 Monaco GP

triggered an incident that ended in killing the Scuderia driver as well as 14 spectators. Clark was so devastated that he considered quitting racing altogether but was talked out of it by Chapman.

Their luck turned soon after as they left behind all these tragedies to scale new heights. Chapman's innovations helped Team Lotus get ahead of its competitors time and again, with Clark making sure that the advantage was not lost. In 1962, he only just lost to team-mate Graham Hill but from 1963 onwards there was simply no stopping him. He won seven of the ten races he entered that year and nailed the drivers' title. He also finished runners-up in the Indy 500. The next season he again finished second with three wins, an oil-leak depriving him of crucial points in the last race as John Surtees won. In 1965, he again stormed to six of ten races entered and took his second championship crown. Such was his dominance that he missed the Monaco GP that season to take part in the Indy 500 and duly won that race as well.

Success eluded Lotus in 1966 thanks to change in engine regulations and he almost quit racing. But he persevered just a tad longer and was finished second in 1967, behind Denny Hulme. In 1968, he won the first race in South Africa and it helped him eclipse Juan Manuel Fangio's record of wins, taking his tally to 25. But three months into the season, his Lotus crashed in a Formula Two race at Hockenheim due to tyre failure and he was killed at age 32, leaving the racing world in utter shock.

FACT

Jim Clark was perhaps the first of the richest Formula One champions. With great wealth coming his way, thanks to his many victories, he lived as a tax exile in Paris and either drove down or flew to races.

John Surtees

Grands Prix: 113
Wins: 6
Pole Positions: 8

Nationality: British
First Race: 1960 Monaco Grand Prix
Last Race: 1972 United States Grand Prix

World Titles: One (1964)
Teams driven for: BRM, Cooper, Ferrari, Honda, Lola, Lotus, McLaren, Surtees

'Everything you need to get that relaxed driving that brings consistency only comes with practice.'

John Surtees is known in motorsport history as the only world champion on both two and four wheels. He was the son of a three-time British sidecar champion Jack Surtees, who also owned a motorcycle shop in London, and as such was always expected to take to motorcycles. He duly did so at age 11 when he first had a bike of his own. At 16, he quit school to become an apprentice at a motorcycle factory and within a year went on to compete and win his first solo race. In 1955 he joined up the Norton works team and won 68 times in 76 races. By the time he was 26, he had won seven world championships with Italian MV Agusta team, from 1956 to 1960. In between, he tested a few cars and entered a Formula Three race at Goodwood, driving a Tyrrell.

His transition was easy and he proved to be as natural a racer with cars. He was first given a drive by Colin Chapman at Team Lotus in the last four races of the 1960 season. He finished second in the British GP and thus invited many offers to drive in Formula One for the next season. He could have very well partnered Jim Clark at Lotus but instead opted to drive a Cooper in his first full season, and then drove a Lola in 1962. This did not bring him any noteworthy success but things looked up for 1963 when Enzo Ferrari signed his as lead driver for the Scuderia. He scored an impressive first victory at Nürburgring but could not challenge for the championship after failing to finish three of the last four races.

1964 began as badly, as he retired in three of the first four races. But another victory in the German GP kick started his title challenge as he went on to win in Italy thereafter. Two more podium finishes meant he closed the points' gap to Jim Clark and Graham Hill. In the finale at Mexico, after Hill had slipped out of contention, Clark's engine blew on the final lap leaving Surtees to finish second and make history with his first F1 title. He should have continued his success story at Ferrari but fell out with the management and quit the team in 1965.

Surtees drove for Cooper in 1966, winning the final race of the season in Mexico. Then he moved on to Honda and helped develop their team for nearly two years. He was justly rewarded for his hard work when he won the 1967 Italian GP at Monza, Ferrari's home race. In 1969, he then raced for BRM and a not so successful season meant he decided to form his own F1 team, following in the footsteps of Jack Brabham and Bruce McLaren. It resulted in an even more frustrating time for him, as in nine F1 seasons, Team Surtees' best results were a second and a third, only the two podium-finishes. In 1973, Surtees retired from racing to concentrate on being a better team owner/manager but he gave that up too in 1978, though not for a lack of trying.

Champion on two and four wheels

FACT

Thanks to his racing exploits with both motorcycles and cars, John Surtees was given a number of nicknames by loving fans. He was known as 'Son of the Wind', 'John the Great', 'Big John' and 'Fearless John' at different times in his career

Denny Hulme

Grands Prix: 112
Wins: 8
Pole Positions: 1

Nationality: New Zealander
First Race: 1965 Monaco Grand Prix
Last Race: 1974 United States Grand Prix

World Titles: One (1967)
Teams driven for: Brabham, McLaren

'Bruce McLaren used to like meeting people. He managed to cope, even when they were asking the most ridiculous questions, whereas my natural reaction was to think "What a bunch of idiots we've got here", and either tell them so or not talk to them at all.'

Hulme just wanted to drive

As a Formula One champion, Denny Hulme stood out in the sense that he hated fame and maintained a low key profile throughout his career. For this curt nature, he was given the nickname 'The Bear', certainly not in keeping with where he hailed from. He was born on 18 June 1936, to parents who lived in New Zealand. His father, Clive, was a war hero and after duty in the Second World War, set up his own farm and trucking business. Denny got his first driving lessons sitting in his father's lap whilst he drove his trucks and by age six, the young boy could drive one on his own. He dropped out of school when he was seventeen to work as a mechanic and driver, hauling cargo on long windy roads.

He first participated in driving skill tests and local races. Then in 1959, his father purchased an F2 Cooper, which his son prepared and raced, finishing joint winner of New Zealand's 'Driver to Europe' scholarship that funded a season racing abroad, in 1960. Denny then moved to London, where fellow Kiwi and F1 driver Bruce McLaren helped him settle down. To finance his racing adventures, he started working as a mechanic with Jack Brabham, who also allowed him to drive his sportscars and single-seaters. In 1963, Denny won seven Formula Junior races and helped Brabham dominated the Formula Two scene the next year. As a much deserved reward, Hulme drove in some non-championship F1 races, before finally making his championship debut at Monaco. He scored his first points at the next race in France but only finished one more time later in the season.

1966 was his first full season and he scored a podium in four races that year, finishing fourth in the championship even as Jack Brabham took the title. The next season, he won his first F1 race at Monaco and then at Nürburgring, retiring only twice and finishing on the podium in every race except once when he finished fourth. It resulted in his first world championship, ahead of his boss. In 1967, he moved on to join his countryman's team McLaren and won twice in Italy and Canada. He was a championship contender till the second last race wherein he crashed at Watkins Glen, eventually finishing third overall.

McLaren slowed down thereafter and he won only the one race in 1969. The following year Bruce was killed in testing and finished fourth in the championship. The team boss's loss showed up and McLaren were woeful in 1971, Hulme not finishing on the podium even once. He was joined at McLaren by friend Peter Revson in 1972 and the team improved a shade with Hulme winning in South Africa. But when Revson left a year later and then died in testing in 1974, Hulme decided it was time to retire from racing. In 1992, Hulme died of a heart attack whilst competing in Australia's Bathurst 1000km touring car race.

FACT

Denny Hulme just wanted to drive and go home. For being so non-cooperative and uncommunicative, he was twice given the 'Lemon Prize' by F1 journalists.

Jackie Stewart

Grands Prix: 100
Wins: 27
Pole Positions: 17

Nationality: British
First Race: 1965 South African Grand Prix
Last Race: 1973 United States Grand Prix

World Titles: Three (1969, 1971, 1973)
Teams driven for: BRM, March, Matra, Tyrrell

'Cornering is like bringing a woman to climax.'

Jackie Stewart's most lasting legacy, apart from his heroics as a race-winning F1 driver and world champion, was his contribution to making the sport a much safer one. He survived a highly inflammable crash at the Belgian GP in 1966, and then took it onto himself to improve the safety standards so that precious lives aren't lost, and that drivers are paid well enough to make up for the grave risks that they undertake.

He was born on June 11, 1939, in Scotland. His father was a garage owner and naturally then the affinity to motoring. But it was his elder brother Jimmy who first took to racing. Meanwhile, young Jackie suffered from dyslexia and left school at age 15. He then took up clay pigeon shooting and was considered a top marksman from Britain, though he failed to make the cut for the 1960 Olympics. He then turned his attention towards racing and from the very beginning displayed in full his special talents while racing in sportscars. Ken Tyrrell then decided to enter him in the 1963 British Formula Three series and Stewart decidedly won seven races in a row.

He joined BRM in 1965 and won a race in his first season, the Italian GP. He finished the season third overall in the championships and was already seen as a future contender by many. He stayed at BRM for another two seasons, winning one more race and finishing thrice on the podium during this time, but failed to repeat his early high-finish in the championship. Then Ken Tyrrell decided to enter F1 and an obvious choice to lead their team was Stewart. It was another of those team-driver partnerships in the sport's history that are the ones to remember. In six seasons with Tyrrell, Stewart garnered 27 race wins and three world championships that put him on a similar pedestal as Juan Manuel Fangio. His record stood till 1987 until broken by Alain Prost

Stewart talks to Ken Tyrrell, 1971

FACT

Jackie Stewart helped introduce full-face helmets and seatbelts for drivers, developed the concept of Grand Prix medical units that travel to races, and successfully campaigned for safety barriers and greater run-off areas to protect spectators as well as drivers

Jochen Rindt

Grands Prix: 62
Wins: 6
Pole Positions: 10

Nationality: Austrian
First Race: 1964 Austrian Grand Prix
Last Race: 1970 Italian Grand Prix

World Titles: One (1970)
Teams driven for: Brabham, Cooper, Lotus

'Nobody knows how long he will live. Because of this fact you have to do as much as you can as fast as you can.'

Rindt took the Red and Gold Lotus to glory

Jochen Rindt was the first posthumous Formula One world champion and tragedy was the essence of both the beginning and the end of his life, so to speak. Born on 18 April 1942, in Germany, he was orphaned as an infant when his parents were killed in a bombing raid. He was brought up by his grandparents in Austria. Count WolfgangVon Trips was his hero and he was bound to enter the world of racing with means available to him to do so.

He started with touring cars and then moved to single-seaters, before purchasing a Formula Two Brabham. He came to England with that car and only in his second race there, he beat Graham Hill, Jim Clark, and Denny Hulme at an event at Crystal Palace. IThat was with Brabham in 1964 but it was just a one off race and for the 1965 season he signed up with Cooper. It was a highly uncompetitive car but in 1966 he finished thrice on the podium, scoring two second and one third place finishes. But race wins still eluded him in 1967 and he grew frustrated, leaving to drive for Brabham at the end of the season. It was a logical move since the team had just won two world championships but in 1968 they had an unreliable car resulting in further frustrations for Rindt. He then moved to Lotus for 1969.

He won his first race at Watkins Glen and eased himself into the team. But he started in 1970 on the backfoot as the new car wasn't ready for him just yet. He started the season in the outdated car but still won in Monaco. Two races later, he had the new car and Rindt laid claim to the world championship with four consecutive victories. Cars had been fitted with aero wings recently, but they didn't prove so safe at first, coming off at high speeds and causing crashes. At some events the practice of removing the wings altogether came into place and for the Italian GP that is what Rindt did with his Lotus. During qualifying though his brakes failed resulting in a crash and his death subsequently. Lotus withdrew from the race and when they returned in the United States, his replacement Emerson Fittipaldi won to confirm Rindt's title posthumously.

FACT

In 1970, Jochen Rindt was shaken by the deaths of his friends Bruce McLaren and Piers Courage. So he promised his wife that if he became world champion, he would retire from racing, but it wasn't to be.

Emerson Fittipaldi

Grands Prix: 149
Wins: 14
Pole Positions: 6

Nationality: Brazilian
First Race: 1970 British Grand Prix
Last Race: 1980 United States Grand Prix

World Titles: Two (1972, 1974)
Teams driven for: Fittipaldi, Lotus, McLaren

'The racing driver's mind has to have the ability to have amazing anticipation, coordination, and reflex. Because of the speed at which the car goes.'

When your father is a well known motorsport journalist, there is certain inevitability about following a career in the same field. In Emerson Fittipaldi's case, it was about racing in Formula One, eventually becoming one of the sport's youngest world champions. Born on 12 December 1946 in Sao Paulo (Brazil), with his elder brother Wilson for company, he overcame his father's reluctance to finance their racing adventures. They started young, establishing a car accessory business and then moving onto building karts, which Emerson also raced. Soon enough, at age 18, he became the Brazilian kart champion. In 1967, they were constructing a Volkswagen-powered Formula Vee single seater, which Emerson eventually drove to championship victory.

This success fuelled further ambition, and he came to England in 1969, where he bought a Formula Ford car and worked as a mechanic to fund his entries in racing. He won three races and then moved to Formula Three, winning the championship that year, despite a late entry. Inevitably, his pace was noticed, and in 1970, Lotus signed him up for their Formula Two team. He continued to impress and Colin Chapman gave him a long term deal, assuring a future in motorsport, before letting him drive the third Lotus car that season, in Formula One. He finished his first race in eighth place and was amongst the points in only his second race, finishing fourth. Jochen Rindt's death later put a dampener on his excellent start, when John Miles walked away from the sport, he became team leader. He went on to score his first victory at Watkins Glen, assuring a posthumous world title for Rindt. But the following season wasn't a good one, he managed to score only three podium finishes. In 1972,, he finished on the podium six times in succession, including three wins, and that was enough to put him in contention for his first title. Then he won back to back races in Austria and Italy, becoming world champion at the age of 25 years and 273 days. His record stood till 2005 when Fernando Alonso broke it after thirty-three years. The next season, in 1973,, he was challenged by Ronnie Peterson and this soured his relations with Lotus. The Brazilian was on track to defend his world title with three wins out of the first four races, and seemed to be getting the better of Jackie Stewart. But at Monza, Peterson took victory ahead of him and that cost him the championship. He then moved to McLaren in 1974. It was a close call that season and he made a late challenge for the title, languishing in fourth at one stage. He finished second in Italy and then won in Canada to go into the final race tied on points with Clay Regazzoni. He finished fourth there even as his title rival struggled and went on to seal his second world title. In 1975 then, he finished second overall to a resurgent Niki Lauda. But this is where it started going downhill for him. He was blinded by family ties as he moved to drive for his brother's F1 team, sponsored by Copersucar. Of course they believed they would be able to recreate the magic of their karting days but that wasn't the case. For five seasons he struggled with the poor cars produced by their stable and often failed to qualify for the races. He finally quit after the 1980 season.

FACT

He was named after an American writer who had nothing to do with motorsport, Ralph Waldo Emerson, admired greatly by his father, Wilson Fittipaldi. But then again, Emerson found all the inspiration needed in his old man's profession.

Niki Lauda

Grands Prix: 173
Wins: 25
Pole Positions: 24

Nationality: Austrian
First Race: 1971 Austrian Grand Prix
Last Race: 1985 Australian Grand Prix

World Titles: Three (1975, 1977, 1984)
Teams driven for: Brabham, BRM, Ferrari, March, McLaren

'There are more important things in life than the world championship, like staying alive.'

The very epitome of Niki Lauda's career was fighting against the odds. And the test began early, almost as soon as he was born on 22 February 1949. He was part of a well established Austrian family, who had built about a strong business and banking dynasty, only to see the young Lauda boy to squander away the riches to pursue a career in racing. He dropped out of university soon enough and enrolled himself in different teams so as to educated himself about what it took to be a racing driver. Then he borrowed money from Austrian banks to fund his passion for racing and bought a Mini in 1968 to go racing in Formula Vee and Formula Three.

In 1971 he took a massive punt, seeking a loan against his life insurance to pay for a seat in the March Formula Two team. The next season it became a first full Formula One drive for him, though results were not as expected. It meant that neither did he move up in the world of F1 nor was he able to pay his debts. He moved to BRM in 1973, hoping to do better, and in the company of Clay Regazzoni ,enjoyed a better season. His reward was a further contract for two years, tying him to the team and in return his debts would be paid off. Regazzoni then moved to Ferrari, and after a glowing reference, Enzo Ferrari decided to pay off BRM to secure Lauda's services, clearing whatever remained of his debts.

His debut season for the Scuderia was error prone, both mechanically and humanly, and despite his first two career wins, he missed out on the title and finished fourth in the championship. But in 1975 all came together for him and he won five races in all, helping Ferrari win their first title after John Surtees in 1964. Lauda could have easily won back to back titles, but disaster struck in 1976 when he was leading the championship by 31 points. At Nürburgring in the German GP, he crashed at high speed and his car burst into flames. He suffered first and third degree burns, broken burns and extensive lung damage, and was clearly taken as dead. But he recovered miraculously and a month later, he was on the starting grid at Monza. He finished fourth in that race.

Heavily scarred, he drove heroically for the remainder of the season and went into the final race at Suzuka with a three point lead over title rival James Hunt. But there was heavy rain on race day and deeming it too dangerous, he withdrew from the event and Hunt took the title. Ferrari were very annoyed with this decision and he endured a difficult relationship with them in 1977. Even so, he won three races and finished on the podium five other times to win his second title and then walked out of the team. He joined Brabham next but won only twice in the next two years, before quitting the sport in frustration. However he returned in 1982 and joined McLaren. He started as slowly as he had finished prior, with only two wins in two seasons but it came together one more time in 1984. Despite never taking pole, he won five races that season and beat his McLaren team-mate Alain Prost to the world title by a mere half point, the narrowest margin in F1 history. After his third title, 1985 was a very slow season and he finished only three races. He retired that year, but stayed actively involved with the sport for a long time to come.

FACT

For all his glory, Niki Lauda was an unsentimental champion. Claiming they were cluttering his home in Austria, he gave away many of his trophies to the local garage in exchange for free car washes.

James Hunt

Grands Prix: 92
Wins: 10
Pole Positions: 14

Nationality: British
First Race: 1973 Monaco Grand Prix
Last Race: 1979 Monaco Grand Prix

World Titles: One (1976)
Teams driven for: Hesketh, March, McLaren, Wolf

'To hell with safety. All I want to do is race.'

Eccentricity was perhaps James Hunt's middle name as he certainly lived up to his reputation. Considered to be the wildest Formula One champions, he was born on August 29, 1947 in London. He was a difficult child to deal with and the fact that he had been blessedly born into a well-to-do stockbroker family didn't do much to calm his tempers. Initially, he had taken to tennis and squash, and met with great success whilst growing up. He witnessed his first race at age 18, a club event at Silverstone and then decided racing would be his calling, becoming the world champion his one dream.

His ambition was met with refusal from his parents who did not support his decision, niether financially, nor morally. He then took to working odd jobs to finance his motives and bought a spent Mini, preparing it himself for racing. Ironically it was later deemed illegal because he used an old lawn chair as the driver's seat. He did not give up and continued to work his way up, paying for his own cars and race entries. His hard work paid off as he found a way first into Formula Ford and then into Formula Three. He developed an affinity for crashing at high speeds which earned him the nickname of 'Hunt the Shunt' alongside.

Given his regular crashes and rough handling of his cars, it was unlikely that he would progress further in the racing world without proper backing. But then that it exactly what happened. Lord Hesketh had set up his own racing team and he was an admirer of the wild child within Hunt. He thought it would be a good idea to have the eccentric racer drive his cars and they started with junior formulae. But at that time costs of running in Formula One were almost the same and they secured an entry in 1973 and Hunt became an F1 driver, somehow. It was the beginning of an eventful adventure, bringing forth two podiums in their first season. Then Hunt finished on the podium three times in 1974 and then a year later, took his first victory in the Dutch GP. He eventually finished fourth in the championship that year, but had to look for an alternate drive as Team Hesketh finally folded up due to lack of finances.

Fortunately for him, Emerson Fittipaldi left McLaren to go drive for his brother's team and it left open the opportunity for him to that seat. It pitched him into contention to be a front runner but Niki Lauda was in superb form that season. He even won the British GP but was later disqualified, falling 35 points behind Lauda. But then the season came to him in the most unexpected manner. Lauda had a horrific crash at Nürburgring and Hunt won that race. He then won again in Canada and USA, and when Lauda miraculously healed to return to racing, his lead had been cut down to just three points. At a very wet finale in Suzuka, the Ferrari driver refused to race and risking his life again, and Hunt drove to third place to take the title in dramatic style.

The following season, he won thrice, but 1978 was a poor season, bereft of any victories. He then left McLaren to drive for Team Wolf in 1979 but after retiring in the Monaco GP, retired from F1 altogether. From 1980 onwards, he took up a commentary stint alongside the legendary Murray Walker and soon earned a respected reputation as pundit. He died of a heart attack at his Wimbledon home in 1993, aged 45.

FACT

Given his eccentric attitude, James Hunt never cared much for safety. During his Formula Ford days, once he crashed into a lake and would probably have drowned if his car had not been fitted with proper seatbelts.

Mario Andretti

Grands Prix: 129 Wins: 12 Pole Positions: 18	Nationality: American First Race: 1968 Italian Grand Prix Last Race: 1982 Caesar's Palace Grand Prix	World Titles: One (1978) Teams driven for: Alfa Romeo, Ferrari, Lotus, March, Parnelli, Williams

'If everything seems under control, you're just not going fast enough.'

Andretti with boss, Colin Chapman: Together they put ground effects to good use

His story is what Hollywood flicks are usually made of; an immigrant rising up the order in America and then returning home to make it big. Only this story played out in the backdrop of motorsport and ended in Mario Andretti becoming only the second American to win a Formula One world championship. He and his twin brother, Aldo, were born on 20 February 1940 in Montona (Italy) even as the Second World War rambled on all around and their early years as a result were spent in refugee camps. After the war ended, they moved with other campmates to Lucca, where he witnessed his first race and decided this was what he wanted to do. He arrived in the USA at age 15 and then began to further nurture his interests in racing. With Aldo, he first started out in local dirt racing events, before moving to sprint, and stock car events by the early sixties. In 1964, he graduated to IndyCar racing.

1965 was his first full season of racing and he grabbed the headlines by finishing third in the Indy 500, on debut, and then duly progressed to win the title that season. A year later, he made it two titles and a third followed in 1969, a year when he also won the Indy 500. By then he had already made his F1 debut, for Lotus towards the end of the 1968 season. From 1969 to 1974, he actively participated in F1 races but did not sign up for any team full time, because he wanted to continue racing in America. It meant that he had to fly across the Atlantic innumerable times and he even incurred a penalty at the 1970 Monaco GP, wherein he was barred from competing.

In 1971, he won his first F1 race on his debut for Ferrari in the South Africa GP, but even that did not deter his plans of not entering the series full time. It was only in 1975 that he decided it was time to compete seriously and signed up with Parnelli for a full season. It wasn't a very successful year and when they shut shop in 1976, he moved back to Lotus, winning the Japanese GP at the end of the season. The next year was an improvement like no other and he won four races, finishing third in the championship. He could have properly challenged for the title but for reliability problems. A year later, in 1978, those problems went away and he won six races to take the driver's title. But the death of his team-mate Ronnie Peterson at Monza meant there were no celebrations.

Andretti remained with Lotus for the next two seasons but could only score the one podium, which wasn't enough and he duly moved to Alfa Romeo in 1981. That didn't bring him any wins either and for 1982, he drove three races for Williams and Ferrari, before retiring from F1. Later, he returned to IndyCars, racing until as late as 2000 in Le Mans 24 Hours.

FACT

In the 2006 animated film 'Cars', Mario Andretti did the voice for a 1967 Ford Fairlane, the car he won the Daytona 500 in 1967.

Jody Scheckter

Grands Prix: 113
Wins: 10
Pole Positions: 4

Nationality: South African
First Race: 1972 United States Grand Prix
Last Race: 1980 United States Grand Prix

World Titles: One (1979)
Teams driven for: Ferrari, McLaren, Tyrrell, Wolf

'This Scheckter has shown himself to be a wise co-ordinator of his own capabilities and potential, a man who plans things with the final result in mind, or for safety. I'm not sure.' – Enzo Ferrari

Jody Scheckter was the last Ferrari world champion before Michael Schumacher came along and he held that dubious record for a wholesome 21 years. He was born on 29 January 1950 in East London (South Africa), where his father owned a Renault dealership and working there as an engineering apprentice, he inevitably learnt to drive at a young age. He knew only one way to drive and that was fast, bordering a touch on the reckless. He was black flagged in his first ever race and it was only a sign of things to come. Soon he matured enough to learn that regular wins would bring him more glory and that resulted in winning the South African Formula Ford championship, and along with it the 'Driver to Europe' scholarship.

Just 18 months after his arrival in Europe, McLaren gave him a drive in the 1972 United States GP and then contracted him to their Formula Two team. As a result, he was given regular chances to drive the third McLaren car during the 1973 F1 season. His reckless behaviour raised suspicion if he could indeed succeed at this level. A prime example was his clash with Emerson Fittipaldi in France and then another crash in the British GP. He was rested for a while but returned later that season at the Canadian GP, clashing again with Tyrrell's Francois Cevert. Despite earning the reputation of a crash kid, Tyrrell signed him on for the 1974 season to replace Jackie Stewart. He had a

The last Ferrari champion before Michael Schumacher came along

topsy-turvy season, not scoring in his first three races and then scoring in eight consecutive races, including winning twice and three podiums. It allowed him to compete for the title but his challenge ended with a broken fuel pipe in the United States GP.

1975 was less successful, with just the one winm and this result was repeated in their 1976 six-wheel car, finishing third in the championship. At the end of the year then, he left and joined with Wolf. He scored a debut win for them in Argentina and then won twice more to challenge for the title again, but eventually finished second behind Niki Lauda. After enduring another poor year in 1978, he finally moved to the Scuderia. 1979 was to be his season as he fended off any challenge from team-mate, Gilles Villeneuve, to score three wins and his first world title came with victory at Monza. The next year was exactly on the other end of the spectrum, as he scored only two points and even failed to qualify for one race as Ferrari were woefully off pace. Considering that his goal of winning the drivers' title had been fulfilled, he retired from the sport.

FACT

Jody Scheckter's elder brother, Ian, also competed in F1 between 1974 and 1977, twenty races in all, though he wasn't allowed to compete in Japan because of their objection to apartheid.

Alan Jones

Grands Prix: 116
Wins: 12
Pole Positions: 6

Nationality: Australian
First Race: 1975 Spanish Grand Prix
Last Race: 1986 Australian Grand Prix

World Titles: One (1980)
Teams driven for: Arrows, Hesketh, Hill, Lola, Shadow, Surtees, Williams

'About as useful as an ashtray on a motorcycle' – Jones on the Lola he drove in his final season in F1 in 1986.

The man who began Williams' journey

Alan Jones is remembered fondly by Formula One fans the world over, but more so by team Williams fans, for he kick-started their rise in motorsport. Born on 2 November 1946, in Melbourne, he was inspired by his father's success, a prominent car dealer who reigned as one of Australia's top racers. Young Alan was kart racing champion at age 15 and soon took to his father's single-seaters. However, his father was bankrupted in Australia's recession, but he still managed to scrape enough cash to fund his move to Europe, in order to further pursue his racing ambitions.

Once in Europe though, he did not have enough money left to finance his race entries and had to return home dejected. Three years later he returned once again, this time managing well enough by selling used cars, and funded his way into Formula Three. Harry Stiller then entered him in Formula Atlantic, and then obtained an entry for him in the 1975 Formula One season, but the team shut shop. Graham Hill's team then took over his contract, and their faith was rewarded when he finished fifth in the German GP. He drove for Surtees in 1976 and finished fourth in Japan, but had differences with the team owner and parted ways thereafter. After the death of Tom Pyrce he landed a drive with team Shadow, and won the Austrian GP, starting from 14th on the grid.

His career changed for the better once he moved to Williams, in 1978, and scored a first podium with his new team, his third overall. The next season, he took it up a further notch winning four out of the last five races and finished third in the drivers' championship. A more reliable car would have helped him challenge for the title and that happened in 1980 when he scored five victories, finishing on the podium ten times in eleven races. He could have defended his championship in 1981 but his rivalry with team-mate Carlos Reutemann cost him, finishing third in the championship. He retired at the end of the season but returned to racing in 1983 with Arrows, and then raced for Lola in 1985 and 1986. Their cars were poor and forced his hand in bidding farewell to F1 for good.

FACT

Ferrari had signed Alan Jones for the 1978 season but they reneged and took on Gilles Villeneuve instead. That led him to the Williams garage, forging their legendary partnership.

Nelson Piquet

Grands Prix: 207 Wins: 23 Pole Positions: 24	Nationality: Brazilian First Race: 1978 German Grand Prix Last Race: 1991 Australian Grand Prix	World Titles: Three (1981, 1983, 1987) Teams driven for: Benetton, Brabham, Ensign, Lotus, McLaren, Williams

'Piquet is just a vile man.' – Nigel Mansell

1987: Nelson Piquet (Williams) at Spa

Never known as a dominant driver but a crafty one, Nelson Piquet used all his talent to win three world championships. Born on 17 August 1952, his upbringing though was far away from motorsport and thus it was a wonder that he scaled those heights. His father was a regional tennis champion and encouraged his son to take up that sport. At age 12, young Nelson was a bright prospect and four years later he was enrolled in a California school to hone his tennis skills. But there he fell in love with racing and returned home to race in karts and sportscars. His family tried to stop him still by enrolling him in university, but he dropped out after a year. In 1971 and 1972 he won the national karting championships and then on advice from Emerson Fittipaldi, bought a Formula Vee and became champion in 1977.

He shifted base to Europe in Formula Three and duly won the British F3 title in 1978, whilst also making his F1 debut in a privately entered Ensign. He drove three more races in a privately entered McLaren and then signed up for Bernie Ecclestone's Brabham in 1979. After Niki Lauda retired, he became team leader. He won three races in 1980, competing for the title that year but an engine failure in Canada meant his championship hopes were dashed. The following season, he won his first world title, though it came only in the last race at Las Vegas where he won from Carlos Reutemann by a narrow one point. In 1982, his Brabham car suffered from unreliable BMW engines though he bounced back the next season to win two of the final three races and secured a second world championship. He stayed at Brabham for two more years but only three wins therein meant he left for Williams.

He expected to be the number one driver there but was given enough competition by Nigel Mansell. Piquet won four races while his team-mate won five races and Williams' management wouldn't give any team orders. They both went into the final round with a chance to win, but a blown tyre for Mansell put paid to his chances, and Piquet made a precautionary controversial stop, handing the title to Alain Prost. In 1987, he started slowly crashing in San Marino and then in retired in Belgium, but finished nine times on the podium including three wins, to win his third drivers' title. He moved over to Lotus thereafter, but after two poor seasons, moved to Benetton in 1990, and won two races. A year later he scored another victory, but with the coming of Michael Schumacher, he retired.

FACT

Nelson Piquet lived up a playboy lifestyle to the hilt, fathering seven children with several different women.

Keke Rosberg

Grands Prix: 128 Wins: 5 Pole Positions: 5	Nationality: Finnish First Race: 1978 South African Grand Prix Last Race: 1986 Australian Grand Prix	World Titles: One (1982) Teams driven for: A.T.S, Fittipaldi, McLaren, Theodore, Williams, Wolf

'I was probably the fastest I'd ever been in my career. I just refused to accept that anybody could beat me and to stay with the turbos I was prepared to take massive risks.' (In 1983)

The original Iceman

A wonderfully aggressive driver, Keke Rosberg was born in Sweden on 6 December 1948 to Finnish parents who were only students at that time. While his father became a veterinarian and his mother a chemist, the both competed in rallies and that fuelled his passion for racing. He soon took to karts, and deviated from his life's aim of being a dentist or a computer programmer to venture into motorsport. He became the European karting champion in 1973 and then moved to Formula Vee. He spent time in that formula till 1978 for a lack of funds, after which he also raced in European Formula Two, North American Formula Atlantic and Formula Pacific series. It was a season wherein he competed in 41 races on 36 weekends across five different continents. That year, he also made his entry into Formula One with the Theodore team and won a non-championship race in the wet at Silverstone. But the championship races were spent in frustration and he even drove for A.T.S that year but with little headway. Later, he moved to Wolf and then drove for Fittipaldi, but despite a podium for the latter team in Argentina in 1980, this time was deemed less of a success. After the Fittipaldi team closed out in 1981, he moved to Williams after Alan Jones retired. 1982 was a highly competitive year when eleven drivers won races and even Rosberg won his first grand prix. But it was the consistent finishes that season which brought him his first world title. 1983 and 1984 were again a bit frustrating due to turbo-engines coming to the fore. But when Williams caught up in 1985, he took pole position at Silverstone with a stunning lap that averaged 160.9 mph, a record that stood until 2002. Rosberg won two races that year to finish third in the championship.

In 1986, he left Williams to join McLaren but Alain Prost comprehensively outdrove him and he took retirement at the end of the season, partly in grief over the death of his close friend Elio de Angelis in testing.

FACT

Keke Rosberg is one of only two drivers to have won the world championship with only one victory, the other being Mike Hawthorn in 1958.

Nigel Mansell

Grands Prix: 191 Wins: 31 Pole Positions: 32	Nationality: British First Race: 1980 Austrian Grand Prix Last Race: 1995 Spanish Grand Prix	World Titles: One (1992) Teams driven for: Ferrari, Lotus, McLaren, Williams

'I get a buzz every time I sit in a racing car, every time I start up the engine ... If I was earning £1 a race, I'd still be a racing driver - just a poor one.'

Mansell always had this urge to drive, still does

It was due to sheer single-minded determination that Nigel Mansell won his one Formula One world championship. Born on 8 August 1953, near Birmingham, he first drove a car in a nearby field at the age seven. Later when he watched Jim Clark win the 1962 British GP in a Lotus at Aintree, he decided that this was what he wanted to do as well. He began as most other drivers did, karting in junior formulae. He worked his way to fund his entries and even survived many crashes to move up in the racing world. One such crash in a Formula Ford testing session left him with a broken neck and there were doubts if he would ever race again. But he did, returning to win the 1977 British Formula Ford title.

He finished fourth in a one-off Formula Three race at Silverstone, after which he sold off his house to finance his entry into Formula One. But he suffered another crash and a serious injury to his vertebrae cast doubts over his career again. Yet he managed to test successfully for Lotus, and made his F1 debut in 1980. He retired from that race but not before a fuel leak caused him severe burns. Overall, he had an unsuccessful time at Lotus, finishing only 24 of the 59 races he started. After the death of Colin Chapman in 1982, he was pushed out of the team in 1984 to make way for Ayrton Senna and he joined Williams. He won his first race in the European GP at Brands Hatch, his 72nd GP start.

In 1986, he won five races and challenged for the title, with the decider in Adelaide. He needed to only finish third and he was doing just that when his tyre exploded, dumping him out of contention. Then, he won another six races in 1987, but he crashed in the penultimate round at Suzuka and suffered spinal concussion, thus missing out on the title once more. Later, when Williams shifted to Judd engines, the cars proved to be unreliable and he endured a disappointing season. He then moved to Ferrari in 1989 and won on debut in Brazil, finishing the season in fourth place. Prost moved to the Scuderia the next year and was given team leader status, which disappointed Mansell a lot. He nearly retired from the sport thereafter before Sir Frank Williams signed him again for 1991. He won five races and finished runners-up to Senna.

Finally, it all fell together in 1992. Williams gave him the best car on the grid and Mansell won the first five races, securing the championship by the eleventh race of the season. In all he won nine races that season and surpassed Jackie Stewart in terms of race wins for any British driver. When Williams signed Prost for 1993, Mansell retired from F1 and went IndyCar racing in America. Following Senna's death, Williams brought Mansell to drive the second car besides David Coulthard and he won in Adelaide. But the team chose Coulthard for 1995, and he instead drove in two races for McLaren before finally retiring.

FACT

Nigel Mansell was the last driver to be personally picked by Enzo Ferrari to drive for the Scuderia.

Alain Prost

Grands Prix: 200
Wins: 51
Pole Positions: 33

Nationality: Brazilian
First Race: 1980 Argentine Grand Prix
Last Race: 1993 Australian Grand Prix

World Titles: Four (1985, 1986, 1989, 1993)
Teams driven for: Ferrari, McLaren, Renault, Williams

'I always work the same way, starting from the beginning of the weekend, so I know at the beginning of the race, from all that I have analysed during the practice, whether I will win the race or not.'

One of the greatest ever drivers in the history of Formula One, Alain Prost was born on 24 February 1955, in Loire region of France. As a young kid, he indulged in wrestling, roller skating and football, almost taking up the latter as a career option. But at age 14, he discovered his passion for racing whilst on a family holiday and turned to karts racing, winning several junior level championships. By 1974, he cast aside his education to become a full time racer,and he paid for it by working as an engine tuner as well as karts distributor. He won the 1975 French senior karting championship and was rewarded with a seat in Formula Renault, wherein he won two titles. It moved him into Formula Three, and in 1978 and 1979, he won both the French and European F3 championships. Needless to say, several Formula One teams had their eye on him but he chose to drive for McLaren in the 1980 season, after having neglected an initial contract from them for 1979.

In his debut season he finished in the points on four occasions but also suffered a number of mechanical failures. Unhappy with McLaren's reliability, he fell out with the management and broke his contract to move to Renault. He won three races in his first season with the French team, including his home grand prix and finished fifth in the championship. Two more wins followed in 1982 and another four in 1983, but he missed out on the title again that year, which was a sore point with the Renault management. He left them and resigned with McLaren for 1984 in a surprise move. It was the start of a dominant period for the team and Prost duly obliged with back to back drivers' titles in 1985 and 1986, a first after Jack Brabham in 1960. In 1987, he surpassed Jackie Stewart's record number of wins and then won seven races in 1988 which should have given him his third title, but for new team-mate Ayrton Senna who won eight races and with them the championship.

This was a prelude to perhaps the most intense rivalry in the history of this sport. The duo battled again in 1989 and Prost started having problems with the management again, leading to a clash between the two at Suzuka, Prost turned into Senna costing him the race and winning his third championship. He then left McLaren to drive for Ferrari and won five races in 1990, heading for the title decider at Suzuka again. This time, Senna drove into him, ending his hopes of a fourth title. After an uncompetitive season with the Scuderia in 1991 he publicly criticised the team and was fired, later taking a sabbatical in 1992. In 1993 he returned to drive for Williams, winning seven races and finally securing that elusive fourth title. Williams signed Senna for the next season and he couldn't bear to be with him in the same team, hence he retired.

In 1997 he bought the Ligier team and renamed it Prost GP. The team proved a less successful venture than his driving career, and folded before the start of the 2002 season.

Krypotonite for Ayrton Senna

FACT

In 1984 Alain Prost lost the championship to Niki Lauda by a mere half point. It was partly triggered by his nemesis Ayrton Senna who almost passed him for the lead in the Monaco GP just as the race was red-flagged halfway through. However had the race been completed, even second place would have been enough to give him the title.

Ayrton Senna

Grands Prix: 162
Wins: 41
Pole Positions: 65

Nationality: Brazilian
First Race: 1984 Brazilian Grand Prix
Last Race: 1994 San Marino Grand Prix

World Titles: Three (1988, 1990, 1991)
Teams driven for: Lotus, McLaren, Toleman, Williams

'I continuously go further and further learning about my own limitations, my body limitation, psychological limitations. It's a way of life for me.'

Looking alone from a talent and ability point of view, Ayrton Senna was perhaps the best driver ever to grace Formula One. His brilliance knew no bounds, especially if the conditions were wet and he could easily push himself to the extremes. He was born on 21 March 1960, into a wealthy Brazilian family. It meant that he never needed to externally fund his racing, a passionate affair that began when his father gifted him a go-kart when he was only four years old. He raced for the first time at age 13 and yes, he won. Eight years later he was racing single-seaters in Britain, winning five championships in three years. He was so taken by the ambition to succeed that he divorced his young wife and let go of his share in his father's business to pursue title glory in F1.

He debuted for Toleman in 1984 and finished second in the wet at Monaco. He would eventually win at the principality six times. He only finished three more races that season and in two of those, he scored a podium. It showed that he had greater talent than Toleman could support and he bought out his contract to move to Lotus in 1985. He scored his debut victory soon enough in Portugal and with another win and four more podiums, he finished fourth in the championship. What caught the eye though were his seven pole positions!

He stayed with Lotus for two more seasons and won four races, before moving to McLaren. It was a great season for him in 1988, when he won eight races in total to take the world championship ahead of team-mate Alain Prost, who won seven races. It was the start of a great rivalry and the two were again contesting for the title next season, such was the supremacy of McLaren. Prost was leading, going into Suzuka and there he turned into Senna, taking him out, and going on to win the championship. Their relationship had reached a breaking point and only Senna remained at McLaren thereafter, the duo not racing for the same team ever again. Prost moved to Ferrari and challenged Senna for the title again. He got pole at Suzuka but had an argument with FIA president Jean-Marie Balestre, accusing him of favouring his French rival. During the race he crashed into Prost and won his second title, but was later nearly banned for the start of the next season.

He won his third title in 1991, this time jousting with Nigel Mansell as Prost endured a tough season. But 1992 was frustrating for Senna himself, as McLaren proved to be unreliable. He wanted to move to Williams but Prost blocked that move in 1993. It led to a heated war of words between the two and when Prost won and Senna finished second, Williams did decide to go for Senna.

Prost retired, but there was a new challenge on the horizon in the form of Michael Schumacher. Meanwhile the 1994 Williams was proving to be a difficult car to drive and despite putting it on pole in the first two races, he failed to finish. Then, at Imola, Senna led Schumacher after an early safety car period and pushed hard immediately after the restart. As he took Tamburello corner on the second lap, the car veered right and hit a concrete wall. The world watched as Senna died, doing what he loved most.

FACT

For all his glory, Niki Lauda was an unsentimental champion. Claiming they were cluttering his home in Austria, he gave away many of his trophies to the local garage in exchange for free car washes.

Michael Schumacher

Grands Prix: 269 (till 2010)
Wins: 91
Pole Positions: 68

Nationality: German
First Race: 1991 Belgian Grand Prix
Last Race:

World Titles: Seven (1994, 1995, 2000, 2001, 2002, 2003, 2004, 2005)
Teams driven for: Jordan-Ford, Benetton, Ferrari, Mercedes GP

'You know the song, 'My Way' (Limp Bizkit)? I think that fits how I feel.' (On his approach to F1)

Michael Schumacher will probably go down in F1 history as its most dominant driver. But that would only be the prelude to his legend. That he was a natural was known by the time he was six years old and had won his first kart race. Born in 1969 to parents who together ran a kart-track in Hurth, West Germany, it wasn't a wonder that he would eventually end up racing professionally. By 1987 he had won the European karting championship and three years later became the German F3 champion. It fast tracked his career that started as a mechanic into a full-time Formula One driver, when he made a sensational debut for Jordan-Ford, at the 1991 Belgian Grand Prix. He qualified seventh and it didn't go unnoticed, even though he retired on the first lap of the race.

Next year, he moved to Benetton and returned to Spa for his first career win. It heralded his partnership with Ross Brawn that would yield great dividends for both in the future. It began here with 18 race wins and two titles in the 1994 and 1995 seasons. But his first championship crown was tainted by allegations that he rammed deliberately into title rival Damon Hill's Williams at the season ending Australian GP and that Benetton were suspected of technical irregularities. But his second title was well worthy as it displayed in full his driving skills. In fact it laid down ground for Ferrari to make a high profile move for him in order to regain glory.

Ferrari at that time were known as a team that had forgotten how to win. Brawn followed him to the Scuderia and together with Jean Todt formed a supreme trinity. Schumacher began with three race wins in 1996 and later five in 1997, battling reliability problems all through. But that was also the year when he was in the championship mix with Jacques Villenueve. It resulted in another near collision when he tried to ram Villenueve's Williams in the final race at Jerez (Spain), an act that was suitably punished with the FIA stripping him of his second-place finish in the championship. It was the worst conduct for any racing driver but at best, it revealed his passion for victory in full, one that was to bring colour soon enough. Subsequently he did finish second in 1998 but a broken leg in 1999 put paid to his hopes. It was now all about to change on his return.

2000 was when he first won a world title with Ferrari, a first for the team since Jody Schekter in 1979, twenty-one years ago. 'Schumi' would then go on to win four more successive titles. In 2002, he won 11 races and finished on the podium in all 17 races. In 2003, with his sixth title, he broke Juan Manuel Fangio's five-decade-old record of five and a year later, he sealed his seventh title by winning an astonishing 13 out of 18 races. It was a prime example of one man's zealousness, his quest for improvement that ground out Ferrari's long term woes and made him a household name in not only all of Italy, but the entire F1 universe.

2005 was the year where he slowed down because of rule changes as Ferrari were beset with problems regarding their Bridgestone tyres. But he was back in contention next year, which was to be his last for Ferrari. In 2006,, he won seven races, but caved to a determined effort from Renault's Fernando Alonso. Even at age thirty-seven, his competitive streak hadn't yet run-out as he parked his Ferrari at Monaco in a manner that prevented anyone from beating his qualifying time. He was penalized of-course, but it showed why the fire would burn in him even after moving away from racing. His retirement would turn out to be temporary eventually and he returned to F1 in 2010 with Mercedes GP, re-aligning once again with Ross Brawn.

FACT

When he was four, Schumacher's father modified his pedal kart, fitting it with a small motorcycle engine. He crashed it into a lamp post

Damon Hill

Grands Prix: 122 Wins: 22 Pole Positions: 20	Nationality: British First Race: 1992 Spanish Grand Prix Last Race: 1999 Japanese Grand Prix	World Titles: One (1996) Teams driven for: Arrows, Brabham, Jordan, Williams

'You should never feel comfortable. There is something wrong if you are. You should always feel under threat, on the edge of your seat and pushing yourself. Win one and you want to win more. It's never-ending.'

Carrying on a legacy: Hill

Damon Hill was born on 17 September 1960, a full two years before his father Graham won his first Formula One world championship. That he would follow into his footsteps soon became an eventuality and as such they remain the only father-son pairing to become F1 champions. As a child he had preferred motorbikes to four-wheeled racing and after the death of father in 1975, he had to work hard to provide for his family. He took up a job as a motorcycle courier and eventually started racing by the time he was 21 years old. But his mother convinced him of the dangers of two-wheelers and just to appease her, he went to the Winfield Racing School in France and gradually made the shift to four-wheel racing. In 1985, he managed to achieve a breakthrough, getting together enough sponsorship to race in Formula Ford.

He won six races and then progressed to Formula Three. Even though he didn't win any races there, he gained a drive in F3000 and took five pole positions to impress Frank Williams who hired him as a test driver, in 1991. A year later, he made his debut for Brabham and in an uncompetitive car managed to qualify for two races. By the end of the season, when Nigel Mansell moved to IndyCar, he was given a race seat at Williams. 1993 was his first full season of racing in F1, and although it came a tad late at the age of 33, he won three races that year to repay the faith shown in him. After Ayrton Senna's death in 1994, he became their lead driver. He was lagging behind Michael Schumacher by nearly thirty points but his disqualification and banning meant Hill was able to close the gap and take the title battle to Suzuka. Here the two rivals collided and Schumacher went on to win, leaving Hill bitter.

He again finished second to Schumacher in 1995, winning only four races in what was clearly the fastest car on the grid. When the German moved to Ferrari in 1996, Hill took advantage of the situation and won four of the first five races in 1996 and won the drivers' title, although he was pushed all the way by his team-mate Jacques Villeneuve. Williams though, decided that it was time to let go, and he moved to Arrows, in what proved to be a miserable year. In 1998, he moved on to Jordan and scored their first ever win at Spa, but a poor 1999 season saw him retire at the end.

FACT

Damon Hill played a guitar solo in the song 'Demolition Man' on the Def Leppard album Euphoria.

Jacques Villeneuve

Grands Prix: 165
Wins: 11
Pole Positions: 13

Nationality: Canadian
First Race: 1996 Australian Grand Prix
Last Race: 2006 German Grand Prix

World Titles: One (1997)
Teams driven for: BAR, BMW, Sauber, Renault, Williams

'My goal is not to be a race-car driver. The reason I'm racing is because I enjoy being in the car and being on the edge.'

Achieving his late father's goal: Villeneuve

Jacques Villeneuve may have lost his father Gilles to a crash in Formula One when he was just 11, but he went on to secure the surname what many would agree is its rightful place on the list of past world champions. He was fifteen when he really started to follow in his father's footsteps, enrolling in the same racing school that Gilles had attended in Quebec. In 1989 he moved in to Italian Formula Three, spending three years there before he headed to the Japanese Formula Three Championship, where he finished second in his debut season in 1992. The following year he returned to North America, where a third place finish in the Formula Atlantic Championship secured him a drive in the Indy Car World Series.

His two years in IndyCar were successful ones, earning the Rookie of the Year accolade in his first season, and then taking the driver's championship in 1995. That led to his move in to Formula One, gaining a seat at Williams alongside Damon Hill. He nearly won on his debut, leading for most of the race at Melbourne before an oil leak caused him to have to settle for second behind Hill. It was a position he also held come the end of the season, with four race wins seeing him take the fight with his team-mate all the way to the final round in Japan.

With Hill leaving Williams, Villeneuve became the number one driver, and seven race wins were enough for him to take the title, despite Michael Schumacher's best attempt to take him out of the deciding race at Jerez. He was unable to defend his crown too vigorously in 1998. However, as an underperforming car saw him only achieve two podium finishes. That disappointment saw Villeneuve leave the team to join newly-founded BAR, who predicted race wins but failed to finish a race until the 12th round of the 1999 season. While the following years saw some improvements, with consecutive 7th places in the championship, the promised victories never materialised. He never got another title-challenging drive, moving to Renault and then Sauber before leaving Formula One, in 2006, to return to America. He stated his desire to return in 2010, but his plans for a seat never came to fruition. He also tried to set up his own team for the 2011 season in a joint venture with Italian team Durango, but again the project proved unsuccessful.

FACT

Away from the tracks, Jacques Villeneuve tried his hand at being a musician. He released an album called 'Private Paradise' in 2007. It sold only 836 copies.

Mika Hakkinen

Grands Prix: 165
Wins: 20
Pole Positions: 26

Nationality: Finnish
First Race: 1991 United States Grand Prix
Last Race: 2001 Japanese Grand Prix

World Titles: Two (1998, 1999)
Teams driven for: Lotus, McLaren

'Formula One is a mind game, no question. You have to think so hard sometimes smoke, comes out your ears!'

Mika Hakkinen first drove a go-kart at the age of five, and promptly had an accident on his very first lap. Undeterred, he continued in karts, and by the time he was 18 he had won five karting championships. He then progressed through single-seater ranks, winning the 1990 British Formula Three title. It was also in 1990 that he had his first encounter of note with Schumacher. In the Macau Grand Prix, he was running in second place behind the German, a position that would be enough to give him an aggregate race win. However, he tried passing Schumacher, and the pair touched, putting Hakkinen out of the race.

The disappointment didn't hamper him though, as he made his Formula One debut the following year. Hakkinen's name became almost synonymous with McLaren, but it was with Lotus that he started his Formula One career, having a strong performance at the first race of 1991, in Phoenix, before his engine failed. Points followed in Hakkinen's third race, when he came in fifth in Imola, but it was to be his only scoring finish of the year as mechanical issues plagued him. The following season was a similar story, and Hakkinen retired from more than a third of his races with Lotus, leading to the switch to McLaren in 1993.

He had to wait for his chance to step up from test driver with the team, but took it with both hands when it came:

The only man who truly challenged Michael Schumacher

out-qualifying his three-time world champion teammate Ayrton Senna on his debut in Portugal. A podium at the following race in Suzuka secured him a race seat for the following year, and with Senna leaving for Williams, Hakkinen became lead driver. Plenty more podiums followed, but that first win proved elusive and looked like it may never come when he crashed in practice at Adelaide in 1995. Emergency treatment on the track saved his life, and he was back in the car for the start of the following season. A strong two years followed, with his first win finally secured at Jerez in 1997.

That win opened the floodgates for Hakkinen. He won the 1998 season-opener at Melbourne, one of eight victories that year as he held off the challenge of Michael Schumacher to be crowned champion at the final round in Japan. Schumacher was sidelined by a broken leg sustained at Silverstone the following season, leaving Eddie Irvine as the closest challenger. Hakkinen's McLaren was less reliable during the 1999 campaign, and the pressure of the title battle was displayed at Monza when he broke down in tears, trackside having spun out of the lead. Again, the season went down to the final race, and victory in Japan meant five wins were enough for him to make it back-to-back titles. However, Schumacher returned to win the championship in 2000 as Ferrari started a period of dominance, and after only two wins in 2001 Hakkinen left the sport.

FACT

Mika Hakkinen showed off his unicycle skills on stage in 1998, performing in a circus in Munich to raise money for starving children.

Fernando Alonso

Grands Prix: 159 (till 2010)
Wins: 26
Pole Positions: 20

Nationality: Spaniard
First Race:
Last Race:

World Titles: Two (2005, 2006)
Teams driven for: Minardi, Renault, McLaren, Ferrari

'Okay, so, Fernando is faster than you. Can you confirm you understood that message?' – Ferrari race-engineer Rob Smedley to Felipe Massa, 2010 German GP

Modern F1's most complete driver

Currently regarded by many as the greatest all-round driver in the sport, two-time champion Fernando Alonso found his spiritual home at Ferrari in 2010. Following a successful period in karts, in which he became world champion, he stepped up to the Euro Open Championship for Nissan in 1999, and won the title. He moved to F3000 the following year, but F1 had already recognised his talents and he landed a testing role with Minardi. He got his first F1 seat with the team in 2001 and put in some impressive performances. In order to further his career he opted to return to a testing role this time with Renault the following year.

Renault rewarded him with a race seat in 2003 and he recorded his first win at the Hungarian Grand Prix just a few months later. In 2005 he became the youngest ever world champion, beating Kimi Raikkonen to the title. Six wins from the first nine races followed in 2006 ,and even though Michael Schumacher kept the pressure on, he could not deny Alonso his second title.

The Spaniard joined McLaren in 2007 and while the opening races of the season went smoothly, it soon became clear that tensions were building between Alonso and team-mate Lewis Hamilton. Unhappy that he had to battle with his own team-mate for success, he finished third in the championship and left McLaren under a cloud to rejoin Renault.

With the undisputed No.1 status he craved in 2008, his second two-year stint with Renault was relatively disappointing with just two wins, one of which included the Crashgate-tainted Singapore Grand Prix. The 2009 package was uncompetitive - he scored just one podium all year - and after months of rumour, he agreed a multi-year deal to join Ferrari in 2010.

FACT

Fernando Alonso is claustrophobic and is terrified of being stuck in a lift.

Kimi Raikkonen

Grands Prix: 157
Wins: 18
Pole Positions: 16

Nationality: Finnish
First Race: 2001 Australian Grand Prix
Last Race: 2009 Abu Dhabi Grand Prix

World Titles: One (2007)
Teams driven for: Sauber, McLaren, Ferrari

'Kimi lives in another world; on another planet. He isolates himself. If he feels pressure, then it's only because he has put it on himself. Nothing that is coming from the outside affects him at all - and that is unbelievable.' – Ferrari team-principal Stefano Domenicali

Nicknamed 'the Iceman', for his cool, unflappable character, Raikkonen showed talent from an early age and made his karting debut at ten. He progressed through the lower formula; Formula Ford, Formula Super A and Formula Renault. In 2000 he won seven out of ten races to win the Formula Renault UK Championship.

His form was enough to merit a test drive with Sauber in September 2000, and he was given a race seat for the 2001 season, with just 23 car races under his belt. Nonetheless, he joined an elite group of drivers to have scored points on their F1 debut, finishing sixth in Melbourne. Raikkonen picked up nine points in his rookie season, and secured a move to McLaren, taking the place of former world champion and fellow Finn, Mika Hakkinen. Despite technical issues blighting his season, he ended the year sixth, enjoying his first ever podium finish at the Australian Grand Prix.

Raikkonen's first race win came in Malaysia in 2003, beating second-placed Rubens Barrichello by an impressive 39 seconds after qualifying seventh. He took ten podium's that season, sealing second place in the drivers' standings, just two points behind Michael Schumacher, who won the title for the sixth time. After a disappointing 2004 season, scoring just 45 points compared to his previous year's 91, 2005 saw Raikkonen win seven races and score 112 points, equalling Alan Prost's 1984 record of the most wins in a season without winning the title.

The Iceman cometh

After five years with McLaren, Raikkonen joined Ferrari in 2007, to replace Michael Schumacher. Far from being nervous about replacing the seven-time world champion, he went on to win the title in his first year at Ferrari, beating Lewis Hamilton by a single point at the final race of the season. However, an investigation into fuel irregularities meant he had to wait nearly a month to be confirmed as champion. He failed to retain his drivers' crown the following year, finishing third behind Hamilton and teammate Felipe Massa. A disappointing 2009 season followed, with the Ferrari struggling for pace in the opening part of the season, he managed just one race victory, in Spa, finishing sixth in the championship. In September 2009 Ferrari confirmed a deal with Alonso, meaning Raikkonen would leave Ferrari with a year remaining on his contract – leaving him to pursue a second career as a rally driver.

FACT

Kimi Raikkonen is allergic to horses. Even so, his wife Jenni Dahlman-Raikkonen owns four of them.

Lewis Hamilton

Grands Prix: 71 (till 2010)
Wins: 14
Pole Positions: 17

Nationality: Canadian
First Race: 2007 Australian Grand Prix
Last Race: 2006 German Grand Prix

World Titles: One (2008)
Teams driven for: McLaren

'It isn't just that he is a driver, he obviously can drive - he is a racer, he can see a gap and he's in it.' – Sir Stirling Moss

Born to be World Champion

Lewis Hamilton took his first steps towards F1 in 1993, aged eight, when he started karting at Rye House Kart Circuit in his home county of Hertfordshire. By ten he was British Champion and on collecting his award at the Autosport Awards Ceremony, the youngster approached McLaren team boss, Ron Dennis, and told him, 'I want to race for you one day.' Dennis wrote in his autograph book that he should 'give him a call in nine years'. Less than three years later Dennis signed Hamilton to the McLaren Mercedes Young Driver Support Programme with the intention of developing him into the ultimate racing driver. The funding enabled Hamilton to progress to single-seaters and the Formula Renault series in 2002, a championship he won in his second year with two rounds remaining. In 2004, he moved up to the Formula 3 Euroseries, and again in his second year took a dominant win. He followed this up by winning the GP2 series at his first attempt in 2006, with Nelson Piquet Jr as his only real opposition. After the departure of Kimi Raikkonen to Ferrari and Juan Pablo Montoya to NASCAR, McLaren found themselves requiring two drivers for the 2007 season. In November the news came that the racing fraternity had long been expecting – Hamilton would drive for McLaren in 2007, alongside Spaniard Fernando Alonso.

Although stunning, Hamilton's first season in Formula One was not without drama. He regularly outperformed reigning world champion Alonso, standing on the podium after each of the first nine races. He scored his first race win in Canada, and followed it up one week later with his second at the US Grand Prix. Leading the championship, Hamilton was now being billed to do the unthinkable and win the world championship at his first attempt.

After a mixed second half to the season, which saw heavy crashes and conflict with Alonso, the teams arrived in Brazil for the final race of the year. Hamilton was leading Alonso and Raikkonen by four and seven points respectively and lined up ahead of both of them on the grid. He could have so easily taken the championship, but a gearbox issue early in the race dropped him down the order and resulted in him missing out on the title by just one point. With Alonso heading back to Renault for the 2008 season, harmony was restored at McLaren. Once more the season went to a final-race decider in Brazil – this time Hamilton arrived with a seven-point advantage and needed to finish in the top five to win the title. As rival Felipe Massa crossed the line to win the race, Hamilton was sixth, but moments later he put in a last-gasp move on Timo Glock - who was struggling on the wrong tyres - to finish fifth and take the title by a point.

FACT

Lewis Hamilton was awarded an MBE by the Queen in the 2009 New Year Honours list.

Jenson Button

Grands Prix: 191 (till 2010) Wins: 9 Pole Positions: 7	Nationality: British First Race: 2000 Australian Grand Prix Last Race: 1993 Australian Grand Prix	World Titles: Four (1985, 1986, 1989, 1993) Teams driven for: BAR, Benetton, Renault, Honda, Williams, BrawnGP, McLaren

'If I'm not winning, I don't give a damn who else is!'

Button celebrates his first victory in 2006 (Hungary) and it wasn't his last

From a very young age, he was earmarked for big things and graduated from karting to grand prix racing in just two years. His skill was obvious from the start, and he was revered by his karting contemporaries Anthony Davidson and Hamilton. Formula Ford was the next proving ground and he duly won the British Championship in his debut season. The following year he moved to Formula 3 and again impressed, catching the eye of some members of the F1 paddock. A successful test with the Prost F1 team led to his name gaining widespread recognition and a number of testing contracts were offered to him. But Frank Williams blew them all out of the water and shocked everyone, including Button, by signing the 20-year-old to become second driver for 2000. A solid rookie year followed, but Williams replaced him with Juan Pablo Montoya for 2001 and Button moved to Benetton. At his new team he had his first experience of driving an uncompetitive car, and was overshadowed by his experienced team-mate Giancarlo Fisichella.

Benetton morphed into Renault in 2002 but by 2003 Button had to make way for Flavio Briatore's protégé Fernando Alonso. However, BAR team principal David Richards still saw potential in the Briton and signed him to partner Jacques Villeneuve, who he went on to outperform and replace as the team leader the following year. His first podium finally came in 2004, along with a pole position at Imola and third place in the championship behind the dominant Ferraris of Michael Schumacher and Rubens Barrichello. Yet, questions were still being asked, as by his 114th race Button still hadn't won a grand prix. Then came the 13th round of the 2006 world championship in Hungary and at last a change of luck. An unexpected rainstorm meant the tight Hungaroring circuit was open for overtaking, allowing him to pick his way through the field from 14th place on the grid to the top step of the podium.

FACT

Jenson Button has a large garage full of exotic cars and is the proud owner of a 1956, split windscreen, Volkswagen campervan.

Sebastian Vettel

Grands Prix: 62 (till 2010)
Wins: 10
Pole Positions: 15

Nationality: German
First Race: 2007 United States Grand Prix
Last Race:

World Titles: One (2010)
Teams driven for: BMW, Toro Rosso, Red Bull

'The chequered flag is really just a stupid wooden stick and a piece of cloth. It's a small thing, but it means so much when you cross the line.'

The youngest ever Formula One world champion, everything about Sebastian Vettel is relative to age. Born on 3 July 1987, he was only four years old, when it became apparent as to where he would be headed in the future. He would keep driving a miniature kart, fitted out by his father, who plied his trade as a carpenter. Then he went on to make his kart racing debut at the age of seven and immediately began winning races and championships. However, there was one obstacle in front of him pursuing this as a full-time career choice and that was money. The problem was solved when he was taken in as part of Red Bull's young driver program.

Ushering in a new era

At age 17, he had already dominated the German Formula BMW championship, winning an unprecedented 18 out of 20 races. BMW Williams signed him up as a test driver by the time he was 18, and at 19, he became a test driver for BMW Sauber. At twenty, he made his F1 debut at Indianapolis, stepping up for the injured Robert Kubica and finishing eighth, becoming the youngest ever driver to score a championship point. Later he became a full-time race driver for the secondary Red Bull team, Scuderia Toro Rosso and raced in the Hungarian GP. There were a number of mistakes in his driving, interspersed with moments of inspired driving such as finishing fourth in the 2007 Chinese GP. But the most cherished moment came in 2008, when he scored his first victory in fine style. At Monza, in the wet, he first score Toro Rosso's first ever pole and then in an equally damp race, went on to register their first ever victory. He was promoted to the Red Bull team for 2009 and immediately seen as a title contender from thereon.

That year he won four races and would have challenged for the title, but for BrawnGP cars running away with the championship owing to a loophole in diffuser rules. The longest F1 season yet in 2010 saw a close fight for the title between Vettel, his team-mate Mark Webber and Ferrari's Fernando Alonso, and it went down to the wire in the last race at Abu Dhabi. Vettel had won five races in all and scored ten other podium positions to stay in contention, and then went on to win the final race of the season which was enough to secure his maiden world title. At age 23 years and 133 days, he became the youngest of thirty-two F1 world champions till date.

FACT

Sebastian Vettel has a knack of naming his cars. He has so far driven Julie (2008), Kate and Kate's Dirty Sister (2009), Luscious Liz and Randy Mandy (2010) and Kinky Kylie (2011).

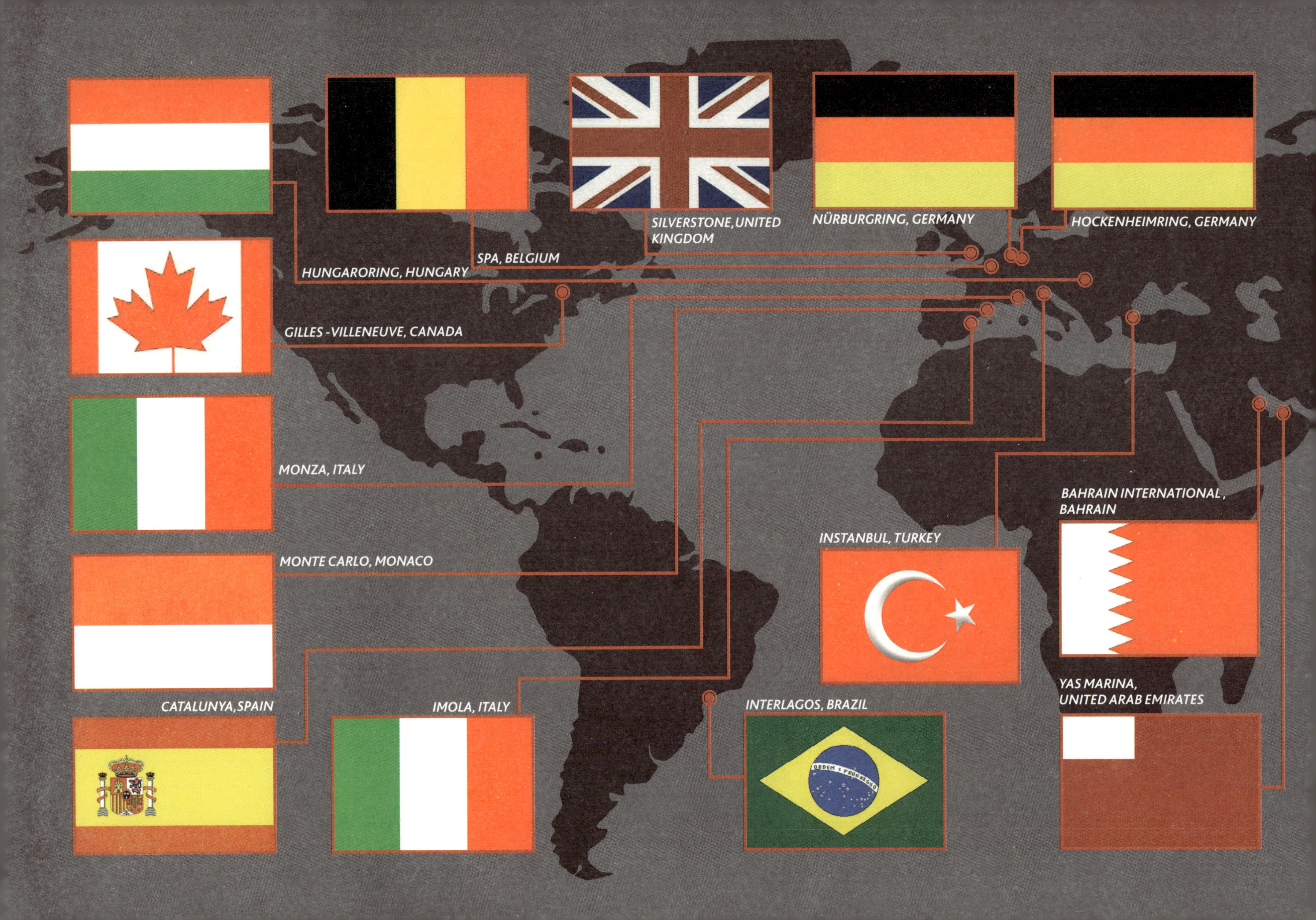
HUNGARORING, HUNGARY
SPA, BELGIUM
SILVERSTONE, UNITED KINGDOM
NÜRBURGRING, GERMANY
HOCKENHEIMRING, GERMANY
GILLES - VILLENEUVE, CANADA
MONZA, ITALY
MONTE CARLO, MONACO
CATALUNYA, SPAIN
IMOLA, ITALY
INTERLAGOS, BRAZIL
INSTANBUL, TURKEY
BAHRAIN INTERNATIONAL, BAHRAIN
YAS MARINA, UNITED ARAB EMIRATES

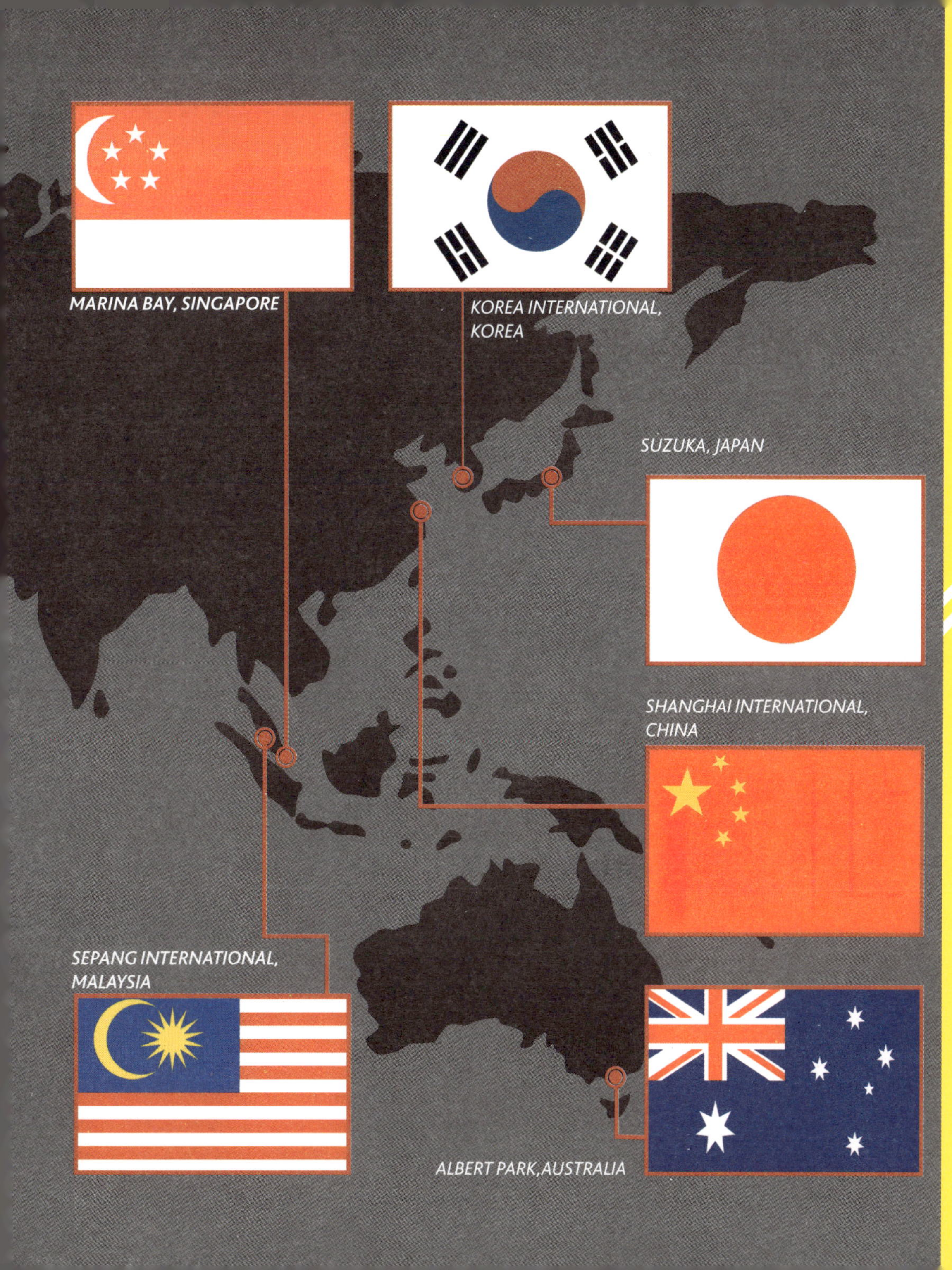

MARINA BAY, SINGAPORE
KOREA INTERNATIONAL, KOREA
SUZUKA, JAPAN
SHANGHAI INTERNATIONAL, CHINA
SEPANG INTERNATIONAL, MALAYSIA
ALBERT PARK, AUSTRALIA

CIRCUITS

Albert Park Circuit, Melbourne, Australia

First Race: 10 March 1996
Years Race Held: 1996 onwards
Length of Circuit: 5.303 km
Race Distance: 307.574 km
Number of Laps: 58
Lap Record: 1:24.125 – Michael Schumacher (Ferrari) in 2004
Most Race Wins: Michael Schumacher (2000, 2001, 2002, and 2004), Ferrari (1999, 2000, 2001, 2002, 2004, and 2007)

On its first inclusion in the FIA World Championship, the Australian Grand Prix was held in Adelaide for just over a decade (1986-1995). The city of Melbourne then fought hard and subsequently won the rights to host this race in 1996. Ever since, Albert Park in the heart of Melbourne has played host to the Australian GP. The street circuit is built around a man-made lake in the middle of Albert Park, with a shuttle-boat moving photographers around vantage points on race-day. The track is well embraced by drivers for its high-speed nature, with cars going flat out for 68 percent of its length.

In 2009, the organizers reached a deal with F1 commercial rights holder Bernie Ecclestone, who had been pushing for a night race here, to stage the event at 5 pm local time. The change is reportedly to take advantage of the new 'twilight' race time, and with the daylight saving zones in Australia and Europe briefly overlapping, meaning higher television audiences.

Bahrain International Circuit, Sakhir, Bahrain

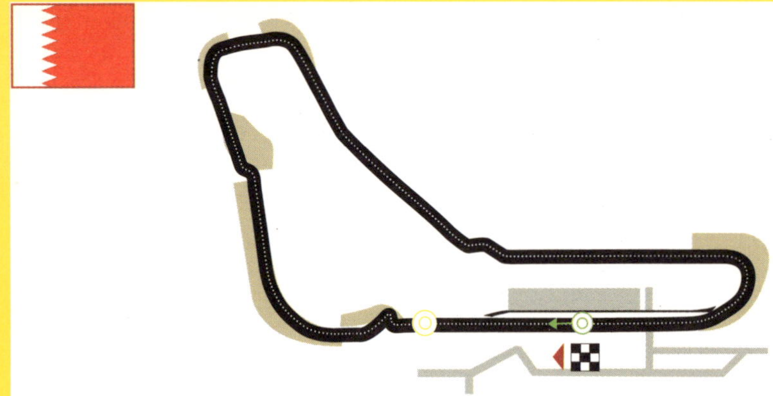

First Race: 4 April 2004
Years Race Held: 2004 onwards, except in 2011 due to political unrest
Length of Circuit: 6.296 km
Race Distance: 308.405 km
Number of Laps: 49
Lap Record: 1:30.252 – Michael Schumacher (Ferrari) in 2004
Most Race Wins: Fernando Alonso (2005, 2006, and 2009), Ferrari (2004, 2007, 2008, and 2010)

In 2004, the Bahrain Grand Prix became the first Formula One race to be held in the Middle East. Half the circuit is modelled on its country's deserts and the remainder has been designed as an oases. The facility has six separate tracks, including a test oval and a drag strip. Built in the middle of the Sakhir desert, by ace designer Hermann Tilke, the circuit posed a unique challenge - that of dust blowing onto the track surface and effecting tyre-grip through the race weekend. They found a solution by spraying special adhesive on the sand around the track, and the mechanics use specially-crafted filters to prevent finer sand particles from reaching the gearboxes. Race winners here don't celebrate with champagne on the podium. Instead, they spray a non-alcoholic rosewater drink known as Waard. For the 2010 season, Bahrain was again the season opener after 2003 and Formula One cars drove the full 6.299 km 'Endurance Circuit' to celebrate the sport's diamond jubilee.

Sepang International Circuit, Kuala Lumpur, Malaysia

First Race: 17 October 1999
Years Race Held: 1999 onwards
Length of Circuit: 5.543 km
Race Distance: 310.408 km
Number of Laps: 56
Lap Record: 1:34.223 – Juan Pablo Montoya (Williams-BMW) in 2004
Most Race Wins: Michael Schumacher (2000, 2001, and 2004), Ferrari (1999, 2000, 2001, 2004, and 2008)

Designed by ace designer Hermann Tilke, the Sepang International Circuit is home to the hottest race of the season. Normally by the end of the race, drivers have been reported to have lost nearly four litres of body fluids. So much so that David Coulthard once famously remarked that 'racing at Sepang was akin to having sex in a sauna!' The track is also one of the most technically challenging ones on the Formula One calendar, and as such then, the event becomes quite an extra-ordinary test for all concerned. Sepang is characterized by two main straights and a couple of small straights interspersed with tight, but high-speed flowing corners. The circuit is quite wide to encourage overtaking and vantage points for spectators are breath-taking. Those on the start/finish straight are able to see the entire first half of the lap and those on the rear side of the grandstand see the entire second half of the lap.

Shanghai International Circuit, Shanghai, China

First Race: 26 September 2004
Years Race Held: 2004 onwards
Length of Circuit: 5.451 km
Race Distance: 305.066 km
Number of Laps: 56
Lap Record: 1:32.238 – Michael Schumacher (Ferrari) in 2004
Most Race Wins: Rubens Barrichello (2004), Fernando Alonso (2005), Michael Schumacher (2006), Kimi Raikkonen (2007), Lewis Hamilton (2008), Sebastien Vettel (2009), Jenson Button (2010), and Ferrari (2004, 2006, 2007)

The Shanghai International Circuit is another on the Formula One calendar designed by ace designer Hermann Tilke. The track is shaped like the Chinese character 'shang' meaning 'high' or 'above', resulting in an unusually long back-straight, that too out of a slow corner and hairpin combination. The circuit is very well known for its stunning architecture – the team buildings are constructed on a special island on a lake on the infield while the main stand seating 29000 spectators provides a view of about eighty percent of the track. The facility was built by 3000 workers working round the clock for 18 months and cost a whopping 240 million USD, becoming the most expensive F1 circuit at the time of completion. In all its existence yet, no F1 driver has won more than once here.

Silverstone Circuit, Northamptonshire-Buckinghamshire, Britain

First Race: 13 May 1950
Years Race Held: 1950-54, 1956, 1958, 1960, 1963, 1965, 1967, 1969, 1971, 1973, 1975, 1977, 1979, 1981, 1983, 1985, 1987 onwards
Length of Circuit: 5.901 km Race
Distance: 306.747 km
Number of Laps: 52
Lap Record: 1:18.739 – Michael Schumacher (Ferrari) in 2004
Most Race Wins: Alain Prost (1983, 1985, 1989, 1990, and 1993); McLaren (1973, 1975, 1977, 1981, 1985, 1988, 1989, 1999, 2000, 2001, 2005, and 2008)

Everything about the Silverstone circuit, the home of the British Grand Prix since 1950, is special. It has a keen sense of history attached to it, for the first ever F1 world championship race was held here. The circuit is built on the site of a World War II Royal Air Force bomber station which opened in 1943. The airfield's three runways, in classic WWII triangle format, lie within the outline of the present track.Owing to a squabble over money, the event was supposed to move to Donnington Park circuit in 2009 but it failed. In slick fashion, the British Racing Drivers' Club under the leadership of former world champion Damon Hill secured the rights for hosting the race for a further seventeen years at Silverstone. This set in motion a host of changes to the circuit, key being the track increasing by a further 760 meters. It will be known as the Arena layout with more emphasis on enhanced safety precautions, new pits and a redeveloped paddock complex to completely modernize the track.

Hockenheimring, Hockenheim, Germany

First Race: 2 August 1970
Years Race Held: 1970, 1977-2006, 2008, 2010
Length of Circuit: 4.574 km
Race Distance: 306.458 km
Number of Laps: 67
Lap Record: 1:13.780 – Kimi Raikkonen (McLaren) in 2004
Most Race Wins: Michael Schumacher (1995, 2002, 2004, and 2006); Ferrari (1977, 1982, 1983, 1985, 1994, 1999, 2000, 2002, 2004, 2006, and 2010)

Situated in the Rhine Valley, the Hockenheimring is one of the flattest Formula One circuits on the calendar, with very little change in elevation. F1 first came to Hockenheim in 1970 as the Nürburgring was getting outdated very quickly in terms of both modern racing and driver safety. When in 1976, Nikki Lauda suffered horrific burns there, the German GP was shifted to this circuit, where it continued to be staged until 2006. The new Nürburgring circuit meanwhile staged the European Grand Prix but when the Valencia street circuit came up, the event was shifted there and it was decided that Hockenheim and Nürburgring would share the German GP, atleast until 2010. After heavy pressure from Bernie Ecclestone, the track was shortened down from its original 6.8 kilometres layout. The modification was carried out by none other than ace designer Hermann Tilke, who had the long runs through the forest undone. Despite arguments that it had lost some of its character, the first race at the new track in 2002, was deemed a great success.

Nürburgring, Nürburg, Germany

First Race: 10 October 1984
Years Race Held: 1984-1985, 1995-2007, 2009
Length of Circuit: 5.148 km
Race Distance: 308.863 km
Number of Laps: 60
Lap Record: 1:29.468 – Michael Schumacher (Ferrari) in 2004
Most Race Wins: Michael Schumacher (1995, 2000, 2001, 2004, and 2006); Ferrari (2000, 2001, 2002, 2004, and 2006)

Not to be confused with the Nordschleife circuit of old, the Nürburgring returned to F1 calendars since 1984, but lost out to Hockenheim for the right to stage the German GP. Since accidents at the old mountainous circuit were increasing alarmingly, Niki Lauda's horrific crash in 1976 raised concerns for driver safety and it was taken off lest changes be made. And when it returned, the new circuit was much shorter than the original 14-mile course, and retained only a small part of the original more-turbulent circuit, though none of the scary features remained. Driver views were clear and run-off areas were in plenty, though rain still continued to make things interesting over the years. The track has hosted the European and Luxembourg GPs with great aplomb, but the track was kept away from F1 for more time in the mid-eighties. But Michael Schumacher's rise made it agonizing to not have two races in Germany. So, it returned as host of the European GP and later in 2009, a deal was agreed to host the German GP alternately with Hockenheim.

Hungaroring, Budapest, Hungary

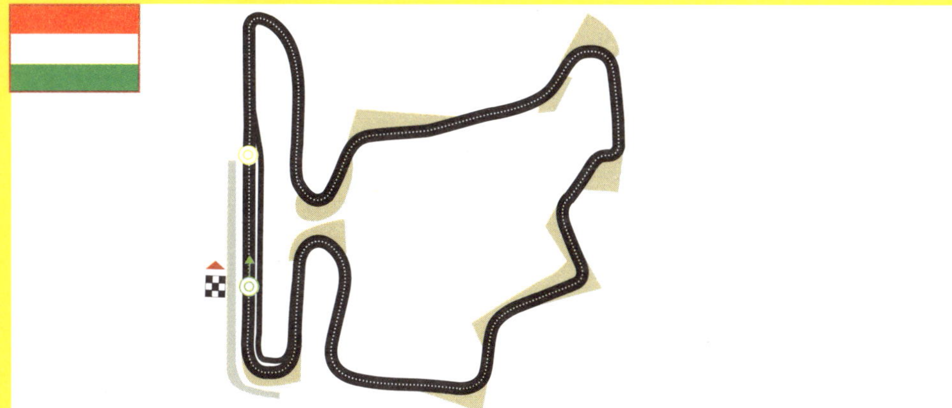

First Race: 10 August 1986
Years Race Held: 1986 onwards
Length of Circuit: 4.381 km
Race Distance: 306.630 km
Number of Laps: 70
Lap Record: 1:19.071 – Michael Schumacher (Ferrari) in 2004
Most Race Wins: Michael Schumacher (1994, 1998, 2001, and 2004); McLaren (1988, 1991, 1992, 1999, 2000, 2005, 2007, 2008, and 2009)

The 1986, the Hungarian Grand Prix was the first Formula One race to take place behind the Iron Curtain, overcoming the political complications of that era. The peculiar nature of the track is such that it is seated in a natural amphitheatre allowing the spectators to view much of the action, from wherever they are seated. Yet, on-track action has left much to be desired for the tight and twisty nature of the circuit doesn't allow for many overtaking manoeuvres. If at all, there are moments to be recalled, they are not many as the race often becomes a procession from start to finish with the first corner proving the best – and only – open opportunity to overtake. Surprisingly the venue didn't see a wet race until 2006 when Jenson Button scored his first victory. Another dramatic moment came when Felipe Massa suffered a horrific crash in 2009, when a loose spring from Rubens Barrichello's BrawnGP car struck him head on. That he returned to race there next season was no less than a miracle.

Circuit de Spa-Francorchamps, Brussels, Belgium

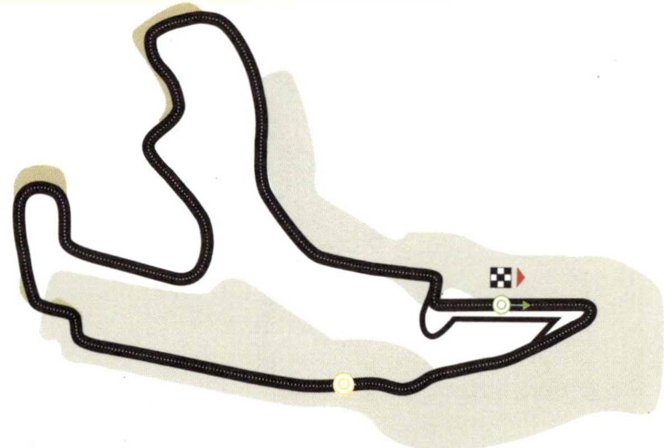

First Race: 2 August 1970
Race years: 1950-56, 1958, 1960-68, 1970, 1983, 1985-2002, 2004-2005, 2007 onwards
Length of Circuit: 7.004 km
Race Distance: 308.052 km
Number of Laps: 44
Lap Record: 1:45.108 – Kimi Raikkonen (McLaren) in 2004
Most Race Wins: Michael Schumacher (1992, 1995, 1996, 1997, 2001, and 2002); Ferrari (1952, 1953, 1956, 1961, 1966, 1996, 1997, 2001, 2002, 2007, 2008, and 2009)

This circuit has been in existence since 1925, and it won't be wrong to say that it is a favourite amongst F1 drivers and fans alike. Since its inception, it has undergone many changes which pruned its length from the initial 15 km to 14 and then to the existent 7.004 km length, though still very much the longest track on the calendar. Even so, it has a characteristic short start-finish straight as also the most spectacular piece of road in the world of F1 – Eau Rouge, a sequence of chicanes where cars attain speeds in excess of 300 km/hr. The cars are pulled uphill and the drivers cannot see the exit of the corner until they are on it, which adds to the thrill and the challenge at the same time. Cars are tuned in for maximum downforce, to keep them railed to the track otherwise they will launch into the air, which is why a shunt here is quite dangerous. Such is the challenge of this circuit that only six men in F1 history have won this race more than twice - Juan Manuel Fangio (three), Damon Hill (three), Kimi Raikkonen (four), Jim Clark (four), Ayrton Senna (five), and Michael Schumacher (six).

Suzuka International Racing Course, Suzuka City, Japan

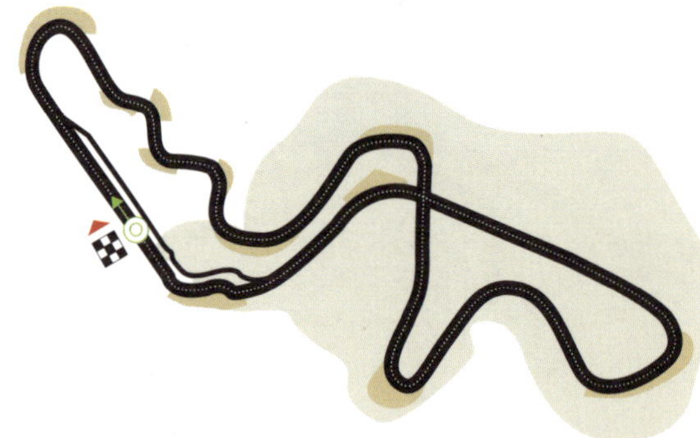

First Race: 24 October 1976
Years Race Held: 1987-2006, 2009 onwards
Length of Circuit: 5.807 km
Race Distance: 307.471 km
Number of Laps: 53
Lap Record: 1:31.540 – Kimi Raikkonen (McLaren) in 2005
Race Winners: Michael Schumacher (1995, 1997, 2000, 2001, 2002 & 2004); Ferrari (1987, 1997, 2000, 2001, 2002, 2003 & 2004)

Over the years, Japanese Grand Prix has been the stage on which many a Formula One championships have been decided. The exact number stands at twelve in 24 races held in Japan, but due to the burgeoning calendar, this is now the fourth last race of the season. In 2009, it was the third last race. In 2011, it will be the fifth-last. Apparently, it will be some time before another championship is decided in this country. The circuit was designed for Honda to be used as a test track, but set inside the boundaries of a fun-fair, it has become a bigger spectacle in the motor racing world. After the first two races were held in 1976 and 1977, the event didn't happen for another decade for want of stringent safety measures, when it returned in 1987. Since then the Suzuka circuit has hosted twenty races at a stretch before Fuji Speedway was awarded the event in 2007, on beckoning from Toyota. In 2008, it was decided that the race would alternate between the two tracks but financial constraints and Toyota's subsequent withdrawal from the sport meant that the race is resting back at its first abode, atleast for the near future.

Korean International Circuit, Yeongam, Korea

First Race: 1 November 2009
Years Race Held: 2009 onwards
Length of Circuit: 5.554 km
Race Distance: 305.355 km
Number of Laps: 55
Lap Record: 1:40.279 – Sebastian Vettel (Red Bull) in 2009
Most Race Wins: Sebastian Vettel (2009 and 2010); Red Bull (2009 and 2010)

The Korean Grand Prix was the latest addition to the Formula One calendar when the inaugural race takes place at Yeongam in autumn of 2010. The race was put on schedule around the same time twelve months prior and since then the parties with vested interests in the 264 million USD deal worked over-time to get everything in place. The race was almost put off as the track wasn't ready on time. But the organizers threw open the track to the public with weeks remaining on the clock, with India's Karun Chandhok getting the honour to drive the first few laps of the circuit in a 2009-spec Red Bull. German designer Hermann Tilke designed the track and it is much like a street-circuit in both design and essence. The track is quite narrow, with tight corners and fast straights, and replete with barriers close to the tarmac, akin to Melbourne or Montreal. The cars race along the harbour side of the province where spectators from the promenade, hotels and yachts can view the race. Part of the city with possible exhibition facilities, shops, restaurants and cafes will be utilized over the coming years to be the pit lane during the Grand Prix weekend, much like Valencia which is also a harbour circuit.

Autodromo Jose Carlos Pace, Interlagos, Brazil

First Race: 11 February 1973
Years Race Held: 1973-1977, 1979-1980, 1990 onwards
Length of Circuit: 4.309 km
Race Distance: 305.909 km
Number of Laps: 71
Lap Record: 1:11.473 – Juan Pablo Montoya (Williams-BMW) in 2004
Most Race Wins: Michael Schumacher (1994, 1995, 2000, and 2002); Ferrari (1976, 1977, 1990, 2000, 2002, 2006, 2007, and 2008)

The Brazilian Grand Prix has been part of Formula One culture since 1973 and was run on 6.92 km long circuit. It was moved to Rio de Janeiro for a decade before the new 4.3 km Interlagos circuit became the sole host from 1990 onwards. The circuit is regarded as one of the most challenging and exciting circuits on the calendar, and along with Spa-Francorchamps, Silverstone, and Suzuka, it is rare in that the circuit in its modern form is one of the few with a lengthy history in the sport not considered to have lost much of its mystique or challenge in its adaptation for the modern, much more safety-conscious era of 21st century F1. Also, it is one of the five anti-clockwise tracks on the current calendar, the other four being in Turkey, Singapore, Korea, and Abu Dhabi. The track features one of the most famous corners on the F1 calendar, the legendary Senna-S. Placed after a quick dash to the first corner, it often plays a big deciding factor in how races pan out here.

Yas Marina Circuit, Abu Dhabi, UAE

First Race: 1 November 2009
Years Race Held: 2009 onwards
Length of Circuit: 5.554 km
Race Distance: 305.355 km
Number of Laps: 55
Lap Record: 1:40.279 – Sebastian Vettel (Red Bull) in 2009
Most Race Wins: Sebastian Vettel (2009 and 2010); Red Bull (2009 and 2010)

Built by ace designer Hermann Tilke, the Abu Dhabi Grand Prix held at the Yas Marina Circuit is the only day-night race in the Formula One calendar. The race starts late in the evening and finishes in darkness. But lights around the track are lit up from the word go, so that that transition from daylight to evening is seamless. The track is built on the Yas Island, intended to be a lap of three parts, featuring long straights before turning into a street-circuit styled section and then finally a Monaco-style harbour front section using public roads called the marina-section. It has three grandstand areas, with part of its pit lane exit running underneath the track. It is surrounded by world class facilities and theme parks all around to provide a complete holiday atmosphere to the spectators. No wonder it is the most expensive circuit in F1 history. Cheered on by nearly 60,000 fans, the cars take to track which features high curbs and ample run off areas, replete with desert sand to give it the UAE feel. Of course, there is also the Yas Hotel, which with its LED lights, giving a breathtaking view to the guests there, just ahead of the start-finish straight.

Autodromo Nazionale, Monza, Italy

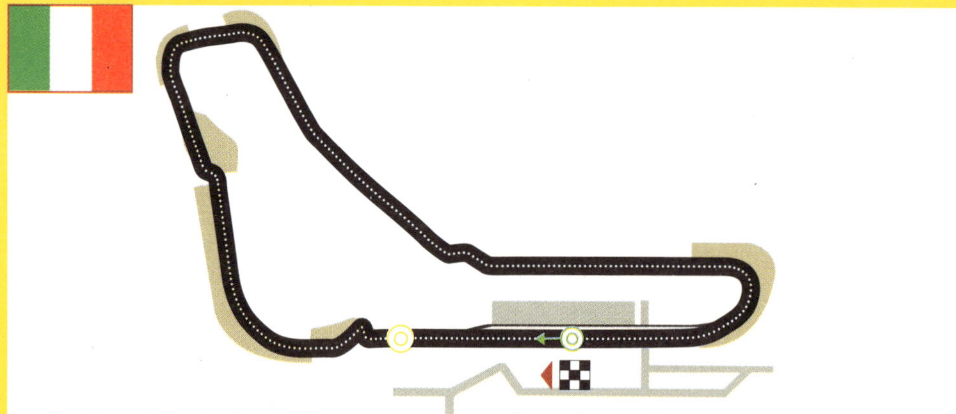

First Race: 3 September 1950
Years Race Held: 1950-1979, 1981 onwards
Length of Circuit: 5.793 km
Race Distance: 306.720 km
Number of Laps: 53
Lap Record: 1:21.046 – Rubens Barrichello (Ferrari) in 2004
Most Race Wins: Michael Schumacher (1996, 1998, 2000, 2003, and 2006); Ferrari (1951, 1952, 1960, 1961, 1964, 1966, 1970, 1975, 1979, 1988, 1996, 1998, 2000, 2002, 2003, 2004, 2006, and 2010)

Like the British GP, the Italian Grand Prix also holds the distinction of being part of the Formula One World Championship since its inception in 1950. As part of a great motor racing heritage, the race at Monza is one which is eagerly awaited every year, for it brings into the picture, the most passionate of F1 fans – the Tifosi. The track was first built in 1922 and it was ten kilometres long. Since then, it has undergone major revamps over the years, and the existing circuit is a mix of fast sweeping corners and long straights. Monza has built its reputation as a circuit which has low downforce requirements, and as such, is more of a high speed drag circuit, with the corners thrown in for measure – its Lesmo bends, the Ascari Chicane, and the Curva Parabolica, provide an awesome test for any driver. They also serve as safeguards against accidents, keeping the high speeds in check, and providing for gravel traps to be set, should the worst happen. This is not just a fool's precaution, because since 1922, nineteen drivers have lost their lives at this circuit while racing in various events.

Marina Bay Street Circuit, Singapore

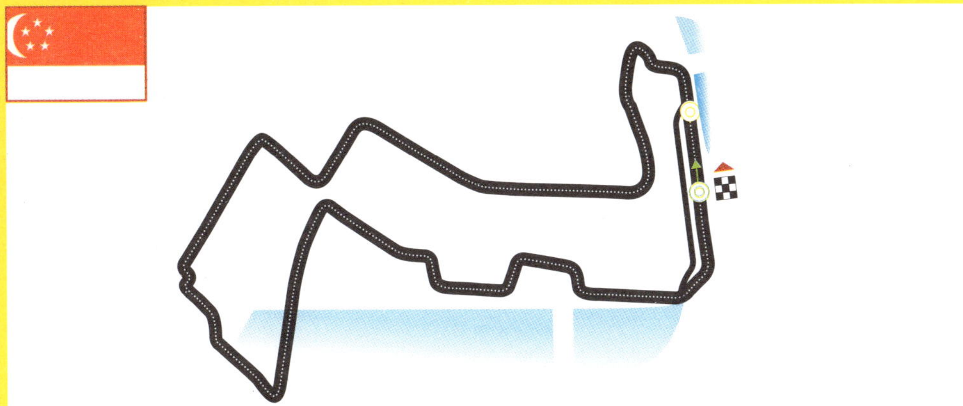

First Race: 28 September 2008
Years Race Held: 2008 onwards
Length of Circuit: 5.073 km
Race Distance: 309.316 km
Number of Laps: 61
Lap Record: 1:45.599 – Kimi Raikkonen (Ferrari) in 2008
Most Race Wins: Fernando Alonso (2008 and 2010); McLaren (2009), Ferrari (2010)

With its inaugural race in 2008, the Singapore GP became the first night race on the Formula One calendar. A street circuit, it incorporates a plethora of 90-degree turns, a mix of slow and fast corners. Two of its stand-out features include the illuminated Anderson Bridge and the section of the track that runs beneath the grandstand at the end of the lap. Here, in front of the world's highest Ferris Wheel, cars accelerate onto the start-finish straight. Using public roads around the Marina Bay area, the circuit utilizes powerful lighting systems to replicate daylight conditions, and the most stringent safety protocols ensure driver and spectator safety. Grandstand seating and hospitality areas lining the track can accommodate more than 80,000 spectators, while a permanent pit area with deluxe paddock facilities is located adjacent to the Singapore Flyer complex. The inaugural race was marred by controversy, as Renault were implicated in crash-gate scandal, perhaps the most disgraceful act in the history of this sport.

Autodromo Enzo e Dino Ferrari, Imole, Italy

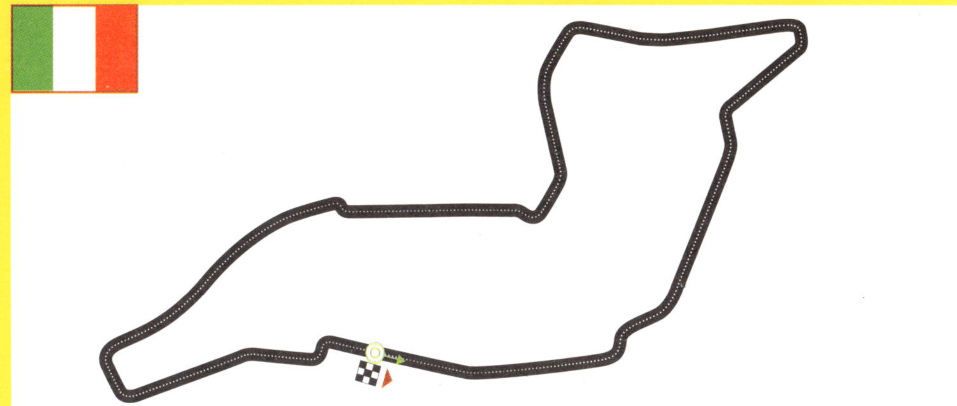

First Race: 3 May 1981
Years Held: 1981-2006
Length of Circuit: 4.959 km
Race Distance: 307.221 km
Number of Laps: 62
Lap Record: 1:20.417 – Michael Schumacher (Ferrari) in 2004
Most Race Wins: Michael Schumacher (1994, 1999, 2000, 2002, 2003, 2004, and 2006); Ferrari (1982, 1983, 1999, 2000, 2002, 2003, 2004, and 2006), Williams (1987, 1990, 1992, 1993, 1995, 1996, 1997, and 2001)

Not so much today, but previously in F1 history, any particular country was allowed to host more than one race. USA, Switzerland and Britain were prime examples, so from 1981, Italy too had two races – the first at Monza and the other at Imola. The area is home to several racing car manufacturers, namely Ferrari, Lamborghini and Maserati, and the track came up in an effort to improve the local economy. Enzo Ferrari sent a first car to be tested here and over the eyars racing action came in spurts. And then came the San Marino GP, staying on the calendar till 2006, when it became impossible to have two races in the same country every year. The track is infamous for three serious accidents in its 1994 event. Rubens Barrichello crashed during practice but survived, though Roland Ratzenberger and Ayrton Senna were not as lucky, crashing and dying during qualifying and the race respectively. However the incident served as a catalyst to make the sport safer. Gradually constructors started complaining about the poor quality of facilities at Imola, and soon after, the event was dropped from the calendar, starting 2007. Perhaps it also had to do with Michael Schumacher quitting at the end of 2006, the Tifosi losing the hero they so worshipped.

Circuit Gilles-Villeneuve, Montreal, Canada

First Race Held: 8 October 1978
Years Race Held: 1978-2008, 2010 onwards
Length of Circuit: 4.361 km
Race Distance: 305.270 km
Number of Laps: 70
Lap Record: 1:13.622 – Rubens Barrichello (Ferrari) in 2004
Most Race Wins: Michael Schumacher (1994, 1997, 1998, 2000, 2002, 2003, and 2004); Ferrari (1978, 1983, 1985, 1995, 1997, 1998, 2000, 2002, 2003, and 2004)

Situated on the Ile Notre-Dame, this circuit gives the impression of a permanent one. But it is constructed every year, with barriers lining up close to the majority of the track. Part-permanent and part-street, it is a mixture of slow and fast corners plus very quick straights. Considered to be traditionally hard on cars and tyres, it is one of the favourites for drivers. The first race here was held in October 1978. Gilles Villeneuve, in his first season with Ferrari, was yet to win an F1 race, but at his home GP, went on to take a memorable debut victory. Following his tragic death in 1982, the track was re-named in his honour. His son, Jacques Villeneuve, never won here during his F1 career. The final corner at this circuit has been famously dubbed the 'Wall of Champions'. As many as eleven champions from different genres of racing have crashed at this corner, names including Michael Schumacher, Jenson Button, Damon Hill and Sebastian Vettel, as also Jacques Villeneuve. Peculiarly, in the weeks leading up to the race weekend, city officials trap as many groundhogs as they can in and around the circuit, and transport the animals to nearby Ile Ste-Helene. Even so, many 'groundhog incidents' have happened over the years.

Circuit de Monaco, Monaco, Monte Carlo

First Race: 21 May 1950
Years Race Held: 1950, 1955 onwards
Length of Circuit: 3.340 km
Race Distance: 260.520 km
Number of Laps: 78
Lap Record: 1:14.439 – Michael Schumacher (Ferrari) in 2004
Most Race Wins: Ayrton Senna (1987, 1989, 1990, 1991, 1992, and 1993); McLaren (1984, 1985, 1986, 1988, 1989, 1990, 1991, 1992, 1993, 1998, 2000, 2002, 2005, 2007, and 2008)

Largely considered to be the 'crown jewel' of any Formula One season, the idea of a race at the principality came to Anthony Noghès, president of the Monegasque car club and close friend of the ruling Grimaldi family. It led to an inaugural race was held in 1929, won by William Grover-Williams driving a Bugatti. The street circuit is put together part by part by a team of engineers, six weeks for building it and another three weeks for dismantling. The work is done once traffic stops on the streets of Monaco, and despite this factor, the circuit outline has undergone little change since the inception of the event a long time ago. Of course, with the changing nature of F1, the requirements of safety have been adhered to. A combination of precision driving, technical excellence and sheer bravery is required to win here, separating men from boys on the grid, as the Armco-barrier lined track leaves no room for error. The cars charge past landmarks, such as Hotel de Paris, the Casino, and then through the tunnel and out around the harbour front, providing a most breathtaking racing event on the motorsport calendar. It is a race every driver dreams of winning and the after-parties are ones to behold.

Circuit De Catalunya, Barcelona, Spain

First Race: 24 September 1991
Years Race Held: 1991 onwards
Length of Circuit: 4.655 km
Race Distance: 307.104 km
Number of Laps: 66
Lap Record: 1:21.670 – Kim Raikkonen (Ferrari) in 2008
Most Race Wins: Michael Schumacher (1995, 1996, 2001, 2002, 2003, and 2004); Ferrari (1996, 2001, 2002, 2003, 2004, 2007, and 2009)

The Circuit de Catalunya was built in 1991, its construction coinciding with the preparations for the 1992 Barcelona Olympics. Not surprisingly, the circuit was part of the games, acting as the start-finish line for the road team trial cycling event. Coming to motorsport though, the circuit is an all-round one, replete with long straights and a lot of corners. So much so, that since its inception, preparations for any new season are deemed incomplete if teams haven't tested here. It is mainly because of the G-forces at this track, testing the cars in and out, telling engineers what is missing where. Even so, come race-day, it is still hard to find a good setup here, since cars can have massive aerodynamic drag and understeer on part of the circuit, while suffering oversteer at other parts of the circuit. It is highly down to the wind here, changing direction at will during a given day, playing a significant part in mixing things up from when the teams test here in the off season and when they actually race. Plus, the track surface is its abrasive and quite bumpy, despite progressive management of the circuit. Tyre wear is therefore quite high and overall it makes for a physically and mechanically taxing race.

Istanbul Park, Istanbul, Turkey

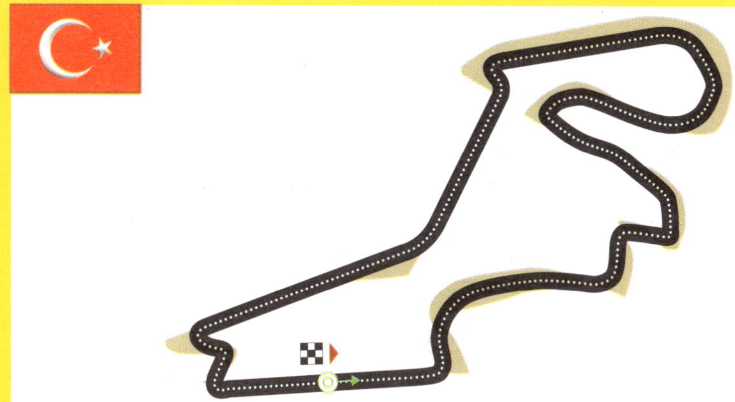

First Race: 21 August 2005
Years Race Held: 2005 onwards
Length of Circuit: 5.338 km
Race Distance: 309.396 km
Number of Laps: 58
Lap Record: 1:24.770 – Juan Pablo Montoya (McLaren) in 2005
Most Race Wins: Felipe Massa (2006, 2007, and 2008); Ferrari (2006, 2007,and 2008)

This track is another in the long list on the F1 calendar to bear the Hermann Tilke mark. Also, this circuit runs anti-clockwise, like in Interlagos, Abu Dhabi, Korea, and Singapore. It wasn't easy to build, for a million cubic metres of rock needed to be blown out to make space and a river running through the hilly site needed diversion. It resulted in the facility being built on four different ground levels, giving it a peculiar character of varying gradient, making difficult for the drivers to come to terms with changing topography. Unlike other Tilke circuits, it doesn't feature longish straights or tight hairpins. But the unpredictability of its gradient mixed with fast, sweeping corners provides an interesting mix for mistakes to happen, thus providing ample chances for overtaking. Turn Eight of this circuit is already part of the F1 legend, nicknamed Diabolica after Curva Parabolica at Monza. The left hander consisting of four apexes is wickedly fast and drivers experience no less than 5Gs for nearly four seconds per lap, making it one the trickiest corners on the calendar.

Marlboro
1
Marlboro
Marlboro
Marlboro

CONSTRUCTORS

Scuderia Ferrari

Nationality: Italian
Base: Maranello, Italy
Active Years: 1950 onwards
Debut: Monaco GP, 1950
Races Competed: 812 (till 2010)
Number of Wins: 215 (till 2010)
Constructors' Titles: Sixteen (1961, 1964, 1975, 1976, 1977, 1979, 1982, 1983, 1999, 2000, 2001, 2002, 2003, 2004, 2007, 2008)

Previous pages: Malaysian GP, 2004: Ferrari pit stop

Scuderia Ferrari came to motorsport, when Alfa Romeo pulled out in the mid-thirties, owing to German dominance and lack of financial resources to keep going. Enzo Ferrari started out with rebadged Alfa cars and by the time the Second World War ended, they had become an institution in themselves. They are Formula One's longest participating team, beginning in 1950, the inaugural season. Ironically though, they did not participate in the first ever F1 race at Silverstone, for their cars were ready only later that year. Even so, in 2010, they celebrated their 60th consecutive year in F1. Jose Froilan Gonzalez recorded Ferrari's first ever F1 victory at the British Grand Prix in 1951, and the following year, Alberto Ascari won the first of back-to-back drivers' championships for the team. Their rivals, McLaren and Williams, would dominate for the next two decades, Ferrari ruing an unprecedented title draught for 21 years. That was broken finally with the coming of Michael Schumacher. After his retirement, Kimi Raikkonen won their last drivers' title in 2007, though their last constructors' win was in 2008.

McLaren Racing Limited

Nationality: British
Base: Woking, Surrey, United Kingdom
Active Years: 1966 onwards
Debut: Monaco GP, 1966
Races Competed: 684 (till 2010)
Number of Wins: 168 (till 2010)
Constructors' Titles: Eight (1974, 1984, 1985, 1988, 1989, 1990, 1991, 1998)

Founded by Kiwi F1 driver, Bruce McLaren, they made their debut in 1966. Since then, the Woking based team has made great strides into the sport's history, considered as an all-time great constructor on par with the likes of Ferrari, Williams and Lotus. They first tasted in 1968 with both Bruce and his team-mate Denny Hulme winning races, finishing second in the constructors' championship. In 1970, McLaren was killed while testing at Goodwood, and it would be two years before they won again. James Hunt gave them a title victory in 1976, and then came an epoch moment for the team. They merged with Ron Dennis' Project 4 Racing and the McLaren F1 team as we know today took off. In 1984, when Niki Lauda partnered Alain Prost, it was the start of glory years for the team, winning double championships in dominant style. Prost then went on to win back-to-back titles in 1985 and 1986. Prost won again in 1989 and then Senna in 1990 and 1991, before their in-team rivalry marked a downward curve. Only in 1998 did they get another taste of championship victory with Mika Hakkinen, repeating it in 1999. While F1 was being dominated by Michael Schumacher, they produced a fast but unreliable car in 2005.

Red Bull Racing

Nationality: Austrian
Base: Milton Keynes, Buckinghamshire, United Kingdom
Active Years: 2005 onwards
Debut: Australian GP, 2005
Races Competed: 107 (till 2010)
Number of Wins: 15 (till 2010)
Constructors' Titles: One (2010)

Red Bull came to Formula One in 2005 after the energy drink company bought out Jaguar Racing in 2004. The selling price was a mere one dollar but Red Bull were contractually bound to invest nearly 400 million dollars in the team. This was done under the leadership of the youngest team principal in F1 history, Christian Horner. They started off well, scoring more points in their first season than Jaguar managed in their last. Their biggest coup was in signing Adrian Newey, who moved over from McLaren in 2006. It wasn't an attractive start though as form fizzled out soon enough, and the team endured a tough 2006 and 2007 season. Powered by Renault, that was also when their first Newey-designed cars took to the track, and in Hungary, Mark Webber finished third while team-mate David Coulthard was fifth. 2008 was even tougher when their secondary team Toro Rosso outraced them consistently. They showed great returns in 2009, winning six races that year and would have been champions but for Brawn GP making good on a loophole in diffuser rules. But 2010 was their year, as Vettel and Webber combined for a total nine wins and their intra-team battle was enough to give them a first constructors' title. Vettel also won a first drivers' championship for the team.

Williams

Nationality: British
Base: Grove, Oxfordshire, UK
Active Years: 1975 onwards
Debut: Argentine GP, 1978
Races Competed: 554 (till 2010)
Number of Wins: 113 (till 2010)
Constructors' Titles: Nine (1980, 1981, 1986, 1987, 1992, 1993, 1994, 1996, 1997)

One of the longest participating teams in Formula One, Williams have had success through innovative designing and using various engine partners. Although they came about in 1975, their first self-produced cars came in 1978 as Sir Frank Williams and Patrick Head formed one of the best known partnerships in the sport. Clay Regazzoni gave them their first victory at the British GP in 1979. The following season, Alan Jones gave them their first drivers' and constructors' titles, retaining the latter in 1981. In 1986, Frank Williams was paralysed in a car crash, but that did not deter the team who won the constructors' title, and Nigel Mansell narrowly missed out on the drivers'. Nelson Piquet though bridged the gap in 1987. All these years they were on Honda power, then moved on to Judd and finally settled for Renault in 1989, which ran through to 1997. His success was replicated next year by Alain Prost, but he was dumped for the mercurial Ayrton Senna. 1996 and 1997 gave them their last double titles, Damon Hill and Jacques Villeneuve being their last champions. Following the end of the privateer era and influx of huge cash by Ferrari, McLaren and the likes, Williams have now been reduced to a mid-rung team.

Mercedes GP

Nationality: German
Base: Brackley, Northamptonshire, UK
Active Years: 1954-1955, 2010 onwards
Debut: French GP, 1954

Races Competed: 30 (till 2010)
Number of Wins: 9 (till 2010)
Constructors' Titles: None

After a good fifty-five years, Mercedes returned to Formula One in 2010 as a works team. They had first come way back in 1954, with their aerodynamically refined cars that Juan Manuel Fangio drove straight to the title. The Silver Arrows won again in 1955, before the Le Mans tragedy that year saw them pulling out. One of their entry cars was directly blamed for triggering the accident that killed 84 spectators. But before they returned as full constructors, they had made a comeback as engine suppliers, first to Sauber in 1994 and then eventually scripting a success story with McLaren. Their return ticket to F1 came courtesy to Ross Brawn. The erstwhile Honda team was rebadged as Brawn GP for the 2009 season and that too at the last possible moment, at a slashed price to keep alive the team. They were powered by Mercedes, enjoying a successful year, thanks to a loophole in diffuser rules, and ran away with both the titles. However, it was apparently clear that the team would struggle to survive on its own and before the turn of the year, their buy-out was announced by Mercedes. It paved the way for an all German team, with Ross Brawn teaming up Nico Rosberg with Michael Schumacher, who returned to F1 in 2010 after a three-year retirement.

Renault

Nationality: French
Base: Enstone, Oxfordshire, UK
Active Years: 1977 onwards
Debut: British GP, 1977

Races Competed: 281 (till 2010)
Number of Wins: 35 (till 2010)
Constructors' Titles: Two (2005, 2006)

Renault has had a turbulent Formula One history, one that dates back to 1977. They brought with them the first turbo engine and soon it would pave for a sensational technological step-up. With the coming of Alain Prost in 1982, their fortunes soared as by next season, he had scored four race wins and helped them finish second in the championship. But in 1985, only two seasons later, they withdrew as full constructors and remained in the sport only as engine suppliers. Williams and Benetton were among their customers and saw great success in the nineties, winning titles in 1992 and 1994, and also in 1995, 1996, and 1997. Despite this, they once more withdrew from the sport, but in 2000 returned after buying out the Benetton team. Their entry was marked as Renault in 2002. Fernando Alonso gave them a first win in 2003 and then went on to give them a first double championship win in 2005, repeating the success in 2006. He left for McLaren in 2007, but returned in 2008 when the team were charged with the crash-gate scandal at Singapore GP and penalized thereafter, with a suspended two-year ban. It resulted in Genii Capital taking over a majority stake in the team, which will now be taken over by Lotus. Renault will go back to engine supplying mode.

Sauber F1

Nationality: Swiss
Base: Hinwil, Switzerland
Active Years: 1993 onwards
Debut: South African GP, 1993
Races Competed: 30 (till 2010)
Number of Wins: Zero (till 2010)
Constructors' Titles: None

Peter Sauber founded a team in his name and they came to Formula One in 1993, having progressed since the seventies through Sportscar championships. All through, they have been a privateer team aided with engines from external suppliers. They have partnered Mercedes (1993-1994), Ford (1995-1996), and Ferrari (1997-2005) previously. But going without a win all this while, they then moved on to BMW in 2005 and formed their most potent partnership yet. BMW had moved on from Williams to form their own team but with little success coming their way in four seasons, they withdrew at the end of 2009. This left the team in a lurch, but Sauber bought it back and entered the 2010 season. However, due to issues with the Concorde Agreement, the team remained as BMW Sauber for the 2010 season, having to wait until the next year to change their name. They reverted to Ferrari for engine supply.

Lotus Racing

Nationality: Malay
Base: Norfolk, UK
Active Years: 1977 onwards
Debut: Bahrain GP, 2010
Races Competed: 18 (till 2010)
Number of Wins: Zero (till 2010)
Constructors' Titles: None

Former FIA president, Max Mosley, introduced cost-cutting measures, after BMW withdrew from the sport after 2009. This opened the path for new teams to enter the championship and one of them was Team Lotus. They are backed by the Malaysian parliament and media, set up by a group of Malaysian businessmen who bought rights to use the Lotus name in F1 from the Lotus Cars owners Proton. But this deal soon ran into hot water with Proton teaming up with Renault at the end of 2010 and challenging their previous deal in court. The license with Lotus Racing had been terminated. After an initial hearing, they were allowed to use Team Lotus bearing atleast for the 2011 season. Team owner, Tony Fernandes, meanwhile, had also bought the British sportscars manufacturer Caterham in case they lost in the courts. They used Cosworth engines in their inaugural year before moving onto Renault in 2010.

Marussia Virgin Racing

Nationality: Russian
Base: Dirrington, Rotherham, South Yorkshire, UK
Active Years: 2010 onwards
Debut: Bahrain GP, 2010

Races Competed: 18 (till 2010)
Number of Wins: Zero (till 2010)
Constructors' Titles: None

Formerly known as Virgin Racing, they made their debut in 2010, after the cost cutting measures had come in place. Their entry was in the name of Manor Grand Prix, but later Richard Branson's Virgin Group came in as title sponsor rebranding the team. Manor Motorsport are a well-known Formula Three team, who helped launch the careers of Kimi Raikkonen and Lewis Hamilton. Later, Marussia took a controlling stake in the team and gained a Russian racing license, becoming the second Russian team in F1 after Midland. When formed as Manor Grand Prix, they had a tie-up with Wirth Research who decided to build the car using CFD techniques. But they split up mid-way through 2011 after it seemingly became clear that the CFD-only approach was not getting them any desired results. The team uses Cosworth engines.

Scuderia Toro Rosso

Nationality: Italian
Base: Faenza, Italy
Active Years: 2006 onwards
Debut: Australian GP, 2006

Races Competed: 88 (till 2010)
Number of Wins: 1 (till 2010)
Constructors' Titles: None

Simply translated to English, Toro Rosso means Red Bull and obviously then they are the secondary team of the energy drinks company. The team came into being in 2005, when Minardi sold it to Dietrich Mateschitz, who also bought Jaguar to turn them to Red Bull Racing. At that time Gerhard Berger was part owner but he sold his stake in 2008. All through these years, they have benefitted greatly from sharing technology and specifications with their senior team, whilst running on Ferrari engines. In 2007, Sebastian Vettel came to the team and he got them a first pole position in the 2008 Italian GP. In wet conditions thereafter he stormed to a first victory, even before Red Bull had scored their first win. Later he would go on to replace David Coulthard at Red Bull and win their first drivers' title, implying that Toro Rosso are always used as a breeding ground for the senior team. Soon after though, it was decided that they would break away from Red Bull and design their own cars. This came into being from 2010 onwards, whence they have been struggling in the mid-field.

HRT F1 Team

Nationality: Spanish
Base: Murcia, Spain
Active Years: 2010 onwards
Debut: Bahrain GP, 2010

Races Competed: 17 (till 2010)
Number of Wins: Zero (till 2010)
Constructors' Titles: None

They were the third team alongside Team Lotus and Virgin Racing to gain an F1 entry in 2010, owing to cost cutting regulations coming in. The team began as a partnership between Campos Racing and Meta Image, and their entry was in the name of Campos Meta. Campos Racing run a team in the European F3 Championship and also previously used to run the GP2 Series team, currently running as Addax Team. But soon after they gained entry to F1, they faced financial trouble, before gaining a shareholder in Jose Ramon Carabante, a Spanish businessman. Italian constructor Dallara built the 2010 cars in Parma, which used Cosworth engines. But their agreement with Dallara fell out midway through the season, for the team did not make any technical progress throughout. India's Karun Chandok made his F1 debut with them in 2010 as also did nephew of former world champion Ayrton Senna, Bruno Senna. Both moved on in 2011 while Narain Karthikeyan, India's first F1 driver, returned with the team after five years.

Team Lotus

Nationality: British
Base: Hethel, Norfolk, UK
Active Years: 1958-1994
Debut: Monaco GP, 1958

Races Competed: 491 (till 1994)
Number of Wins: 79 (till 1994)
Constructors' Titles: Seven (1963, 1965, 1968, 1970, 1972, 1973, 1978)

Perhaps one of the greatest minds in Formula One history, Colin Chapman founded Lotus Engineering in 1952. Later he formed Team Lotus, a separate entity for racing in F1 and that was in 1954, with their first entry coming in 1958. This had been due to Formula Two regulations taking precedence in 1956 and 1957 when a large number of sportscar and private entries found their way into the championship. Innes Ireland got them their first F1 victory in the 1961, USGP but two years later, Jim Clark drove the Lotus 25 to seven wins in a season and the double world championships. He dominated again in 1965, this time with the Lotus 33. Later, their black-gold livery would go on to become a timeless classic. After the wings came gas-turbine powered cars, the four wheel drive cars and then eventually the ground-effects car, which allowed drivers such as Jochen Rindt, Emerson Fitiipaldi and Mario Andretti. Buoyed by this technological uprising, Team Lotus were the first to achieve 50 Grand Prix victories. After Chapman's death began the downward spiral as the team searched for form in the eighties, first with Nigel Mansell, and then with Ayrton Senna. With the arrival of the nineties, the team was beginning to run into financial problems, and it finally folded up in 1994.

Brabham Racing

Nationality: British
Base: Milton Keynes, United Kingdom
Active Years: 1962-1992
Debut: German GP, 1962
Races Competed: 394
Number of Wins: 35
Constructors' Titles: Two (1966, 1967)

Even today, Jack Brabham remains the only F1 driver to win the World Championship in a car bearing his own name. That happened after his double championship wins for Cooper in 1959 and 1960, when he returned home to Australia, forming a partnership with his engineer friend Ron Tauranac. They came to England and set up Motor Racing Developments (MRD), later renamed Brabham. They first raced in 1964, and Dan Gurney brought them two victories that season. By 1965, a new engine formula was introduced and Brabham used Repco engines to storm to the front of the grid. It secured him his third world title, and history was made. Denny Hulme repeated their success in 1966. Later, with more developed teams coming to the fore, at age 44, Brabham left the sport after 1970 and would only take part as team-owner. Later in 1971, the team was sold to Bernie Ecclestone. Though a title drought followed, Nelson Piquet joined the team in 1978 and won in both 1981 and 1983. But when he left in 1985, it brought a rapid downcurve for them, and they withdrew from competition in 1988. A Swiss financier bought the team in 1989, but did their name no good for the next three years and finally folded up in 1992.

Alfa Romeo

Nationality: Italian
Base: Milan, Italy
Active Years: 1950-1951, 1979-1985
Debut: British GP, 1950
Races Competed: 110
Number of Wins: 10
Constructors' Titles: None

Alfa Romeo's name is synonymous with the rise of motorsport in the pre-First World War era, and they sprang to greatness in the 1920 and 1930s, racing across Europe. Their P2 car was the standard setter all along and drivers like Antonio Ascari and Tazio Nuvolari raced this machinery with great aplomb. Between 1932 and 1934, Nuvolari won every race he entered, and is remembered as one of the best ever drivers. In 1933, Alfa Romeo was nationalized and officially withdrew from the sport, although Scuderia Ferrari under Enzo Ferrari continued to field their cars. They gave strong competition to Mercedes and Auto Union in the years leading to the Second World War, before Alfa again started racing in 1938. When the war got over, they won 46 straight races with a car designed before hostilities broke out. That same car, now redefined as per Formula One regulations, took Nino Farina to the inaugural championship in 1950 and then a year later, Juan Manuel Fangio repeated the feat. Later that year, they left F1 to concentrate on sportscar racing. They returned in the mid-seventies as an engine supplier, before becoming a full time constructor again in 1979. But their comeback was short lived and they left mid-way through the eighties.

Maserati

Nationality: Italian
Base: Modena, Italy
Active Years: 1950-1960
Debut: British GP, 1950
Races Competed: 71
Number of Wins: 9
Constructors' Titles: None

Involved in Italian motorsport since the early 1900s, the marquee was founded by the Maserati brothers, who were into making spark plugs before the First World War. Racing came to them as soon as hostilities ended and 1926, when they first won a race. Their rivalry with Alfa Romeo was written gloriously in the 1930s and one of their key drivers turned out to be Tazio Nuvolari. The rise of German Engineering saw Maserati lose out, before rising again after moving base from Bologna to Modena in 1940. Soon after the Second World War, the brothers worked on a sportscar whose engine was based on Formula One specification, and they came to the championship amidst Alfa Romeo and Ferrari domination in the early years. Juan Manuel Fangio won a first F1 race for Maserati at the 1953 Italian Grand Prix. He continued to drive for them in 1954, while waiting for Mercedes to bring out their car. Their best known car, the 250F, was a hit with privateers and indeed, Fangio and Stirling Moss were amongst the first beneficiaries. The latter won two races in 1956 but it was Fangio who hit the headlines with four wins in 1957, winning his fifth drivers' title. By the end of that season however, they were in deep financial troubles and by 1958, the factory team was no more.

Cooper

Nationality: British
Base: Surbiton, Surrey, UK
Active Years: 1950-1969
Debut: British GP, 1950
Races Competed: 129
Number of Wins: 16
Constructors' Titles: Two (1959, 1960)

Charles Cooper, a racing mechanic, built a 500cc motorcycle-engine racing car for his son John and the Cooper Car Company was born. Post the Second World War, they built more on this formula, qualifying for the inaugural season of the Formula One world championship in 1950. But from there on, they started working on a mid-engine concept and the first such car was raced by Jack Brabham in 1955. Two seasons later, a new engine formula was to be adopted and they put together a chassis mated with a Climax engine. Although the 1957 car handled better, they were grossly underpowered. Then in 1958, Rob Walker ordered a more powerful Climax engine for them and Stirling Moss duly drove it to victory at the Argentine GP, a first victory for a rear-engine cars. It showed great promise for the idea and they invested more into it, bringing out the T51 for 1959. Developed by John Cooper and Brabham, it had a 2.5 litre Climax engine giving a power boost and delivering two back to back world championships in 1959 and 1960. However, other constructors copied the idea and developed better machines, setting them on a downward spiral. Cooper then disappeared from F1 in 1968.

ISBN: 978-81-7436-868-3

Published in India by Roli Books
M-75, G.K. II Market;
New Delhi-110 048, India.
Phone: ++91-11- 29212271, 40682000
Fax: ++91-11-29217185
Email: info@rolibooks.com
Website: rolibooks.com

Design: Devan Das
Editor: Aditi Ghosh
Production: Shaji Sahadevan

Printed and bound in India by EIH Press, New Delhi

Photo Credits:

Corbis: Pages 2, 4, 6-7, 8, 18-19, 20-21, 25, 29, 43, 51, 56-57, 65, 68-69, 73, 76-77, 78, 83, 84, 85, 88, 89, 92, 93, 96-97, 98, 100, 104, 105, 106, 107, 108, 109, 110, 111, 112, 117, 118, 119, 120, 122, 123, 124, 125, 126, 130, 131, 132, 133, 134, 135, 148-149, 150, 151, 152, 153, 154, 155, 156, 157, and 159

Getty Images: Pages 9, 10, 11, 12-13, 14, 15, 16, 22-23, 24, 26, 28, 30-31, 34, 49, 59, 60, 61, 64, 71, 72, 79, 86, 87, 91, 102-103, 113, 115, 116, 124, 127, 128, 129, 133, 151, and 155

LAT Photographic Digital Archive: Pages 32-33, 35, 36, 37, 38-39, 40, 41, 42, 44, 46-47, 48, 50, 52-53, 58, 59, 61, 62, 63, 65, 70, 73, 74, 80, 89, 90, 93, 99, 104, 112, 114, 119, 121, 122, 128, and 129

Facing page: Formula One racecars representing 30 years of Cosworth engines entered in Formula One races (Front to back: Lotus 49 from 1967, Tyrrell from 1970, Lotus from 1971, Tyrrell from 1973, Lotus from 1977, Tyrrell from 1983, Brabham from 1981, Lotus from 1983, Williams from 1983, and the Stewart from 1997)

TEAM LOTUS
6
1
REINE WISELL
GOLD LEA
TEAM LO
5
elf
L.LEROY
John Player Special
Valvoline